The Greatest Love Coloring Book

Of Hearts and Heart Designs

By
Mary Beth Brace

Copyright 2017

ISBN-13: 978-1542552783

ISBN – 10: 1542552788

Thank you for choosing The Greatest Love Coloring Book. I enjoyed making the hearts. Reading other reviews from similar coloring books, I noticed that more detail was wanted, so I went back through this coloring book and added more patterns. It's a balancing act, I'm finding, to get things just right for everyone. I chose a balance between simple and complex.

I've included the words of my song, "The Greatest Love" in the coloring book. It is based on 1 Corinthians 13, the love chapter. There are phrases of the song on the back of each picture, but up high on the page so they won't be a distraction. The 48 phrases of the song were my guide as to how many hearts I would put into the coloring book.

Other Coloring books that I've completed and for sale on Amazon:

Horse Lover's Coloring Book 1

Horse Lover's Coloring Book 2

Happy Coloring!

Mary Beth

marybethbrace@gmail.com

This blank page is for your convenience to test your pens. Place a piece of cardstock behind coloring page if ink bleeds through paper.

If I could sing with the voice of an angel,

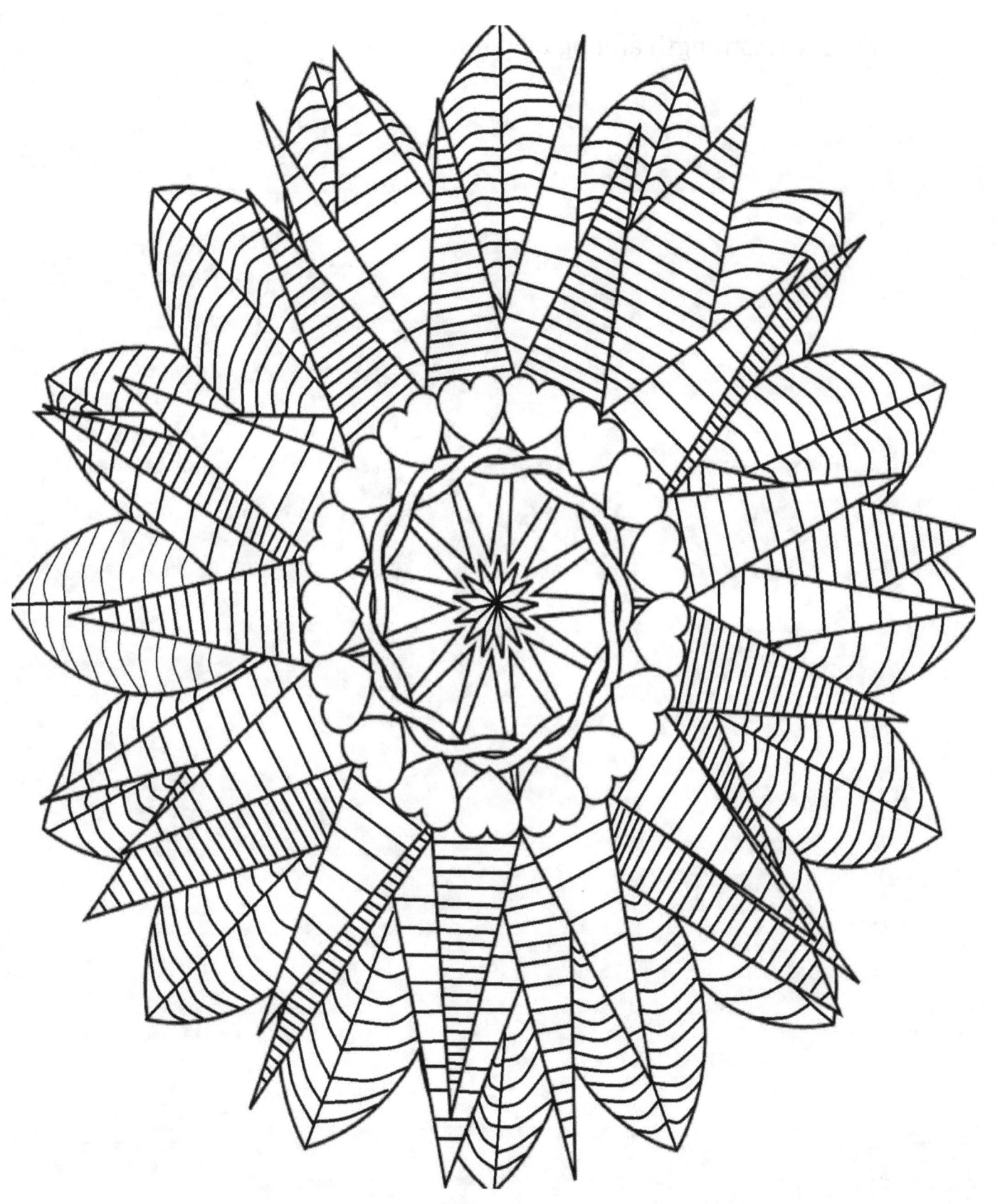

Debate with strength among all men,

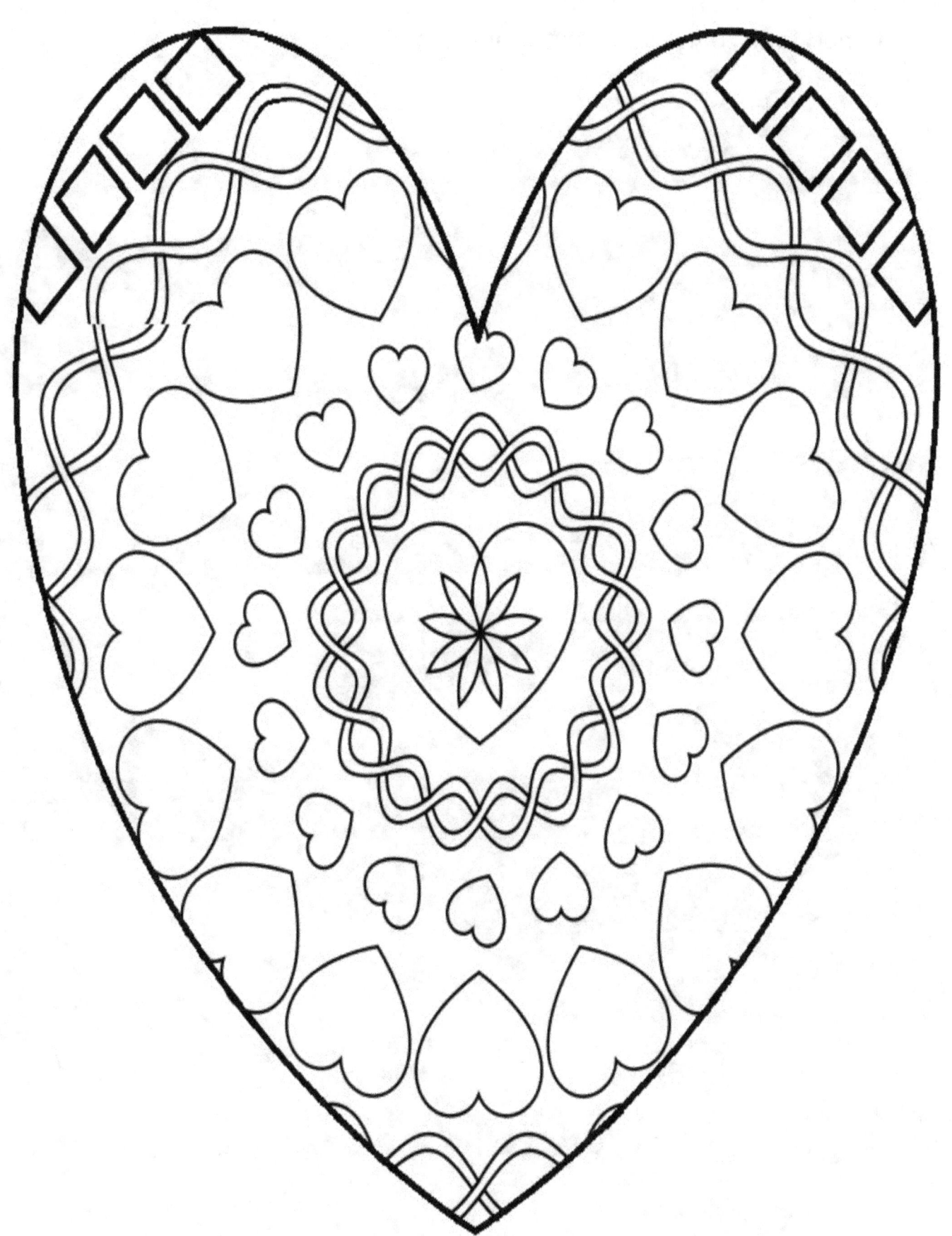

If I had faith to move a great mountain,

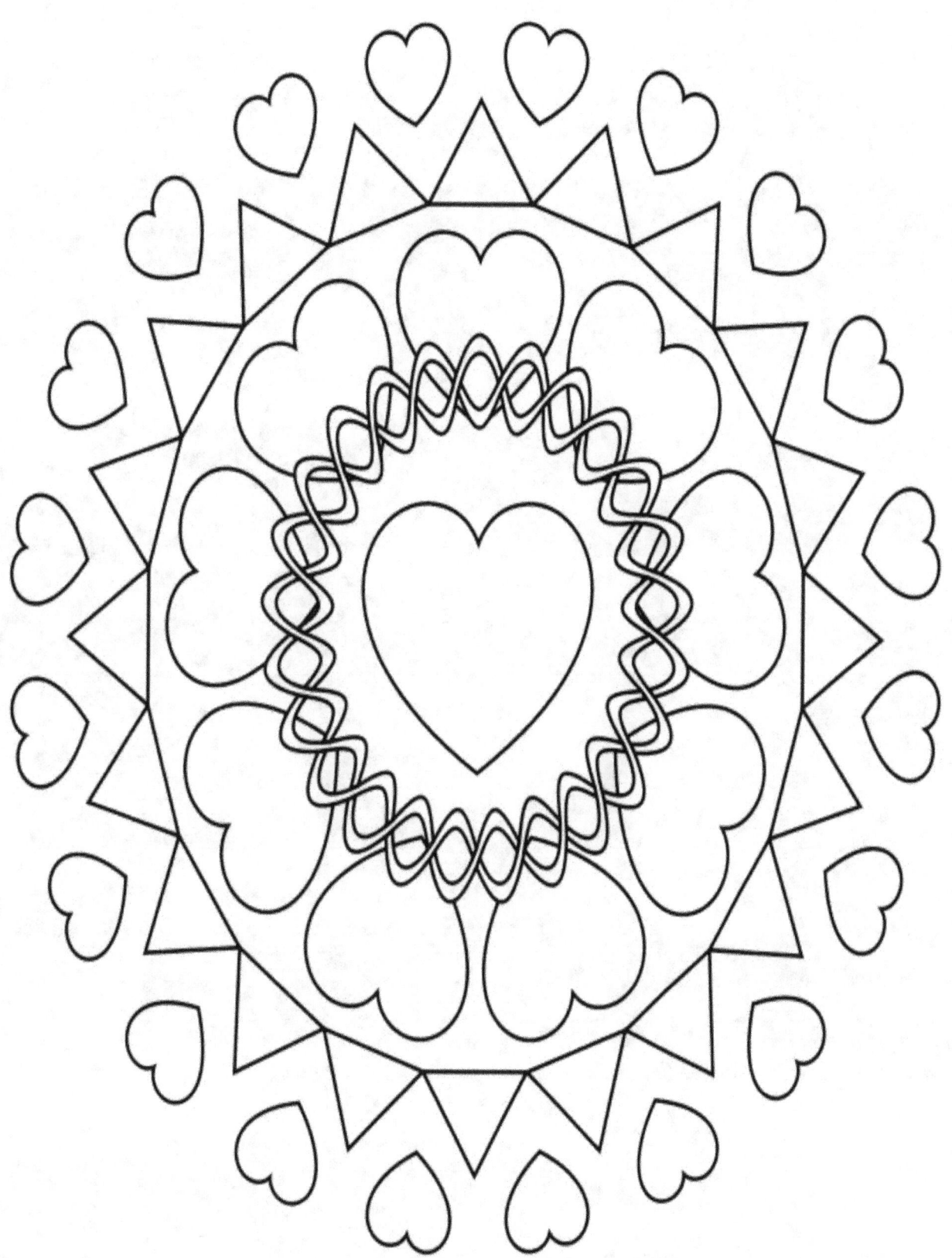

But had not love, what then?

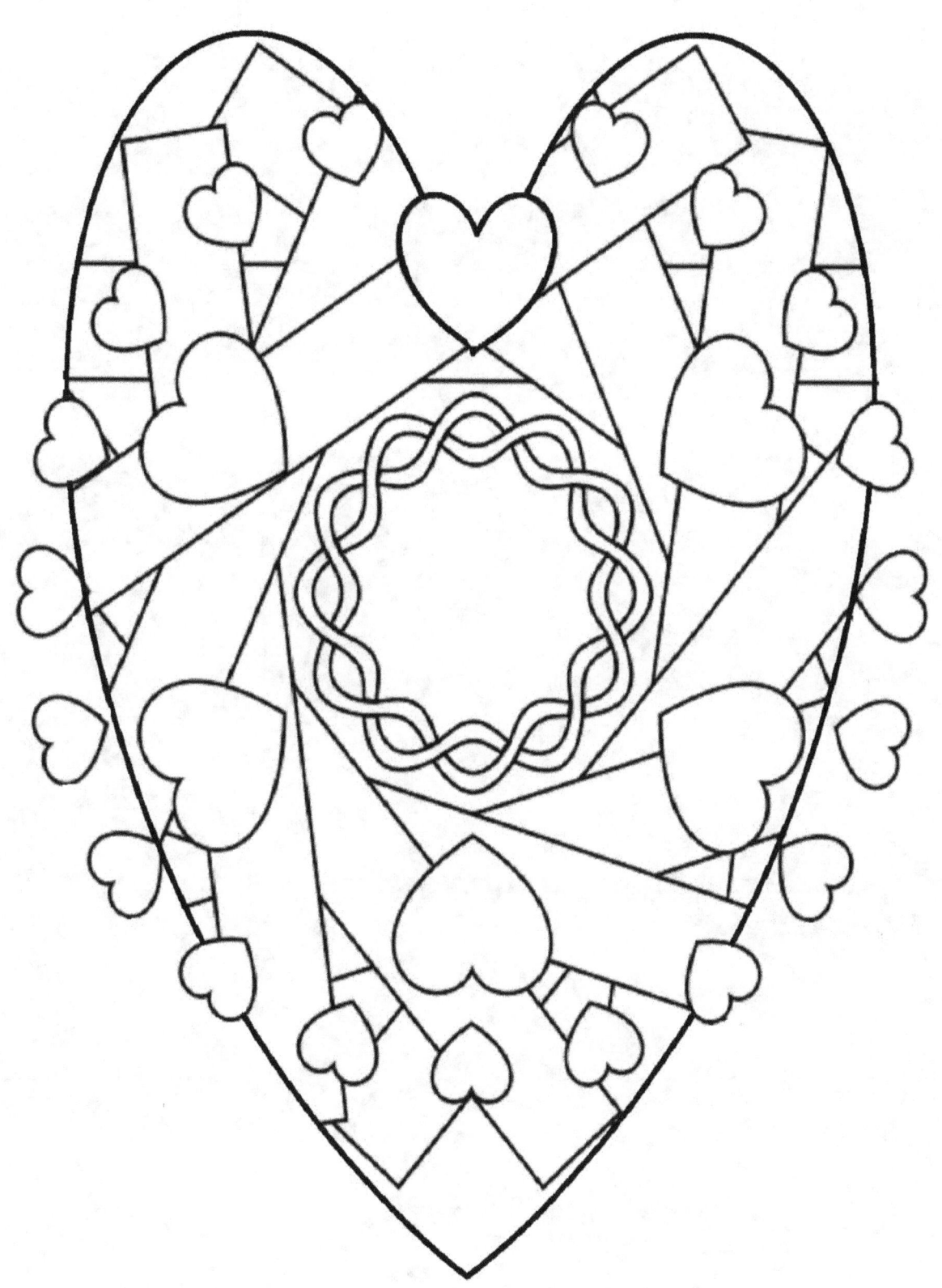

What does it profit if love is not winning?

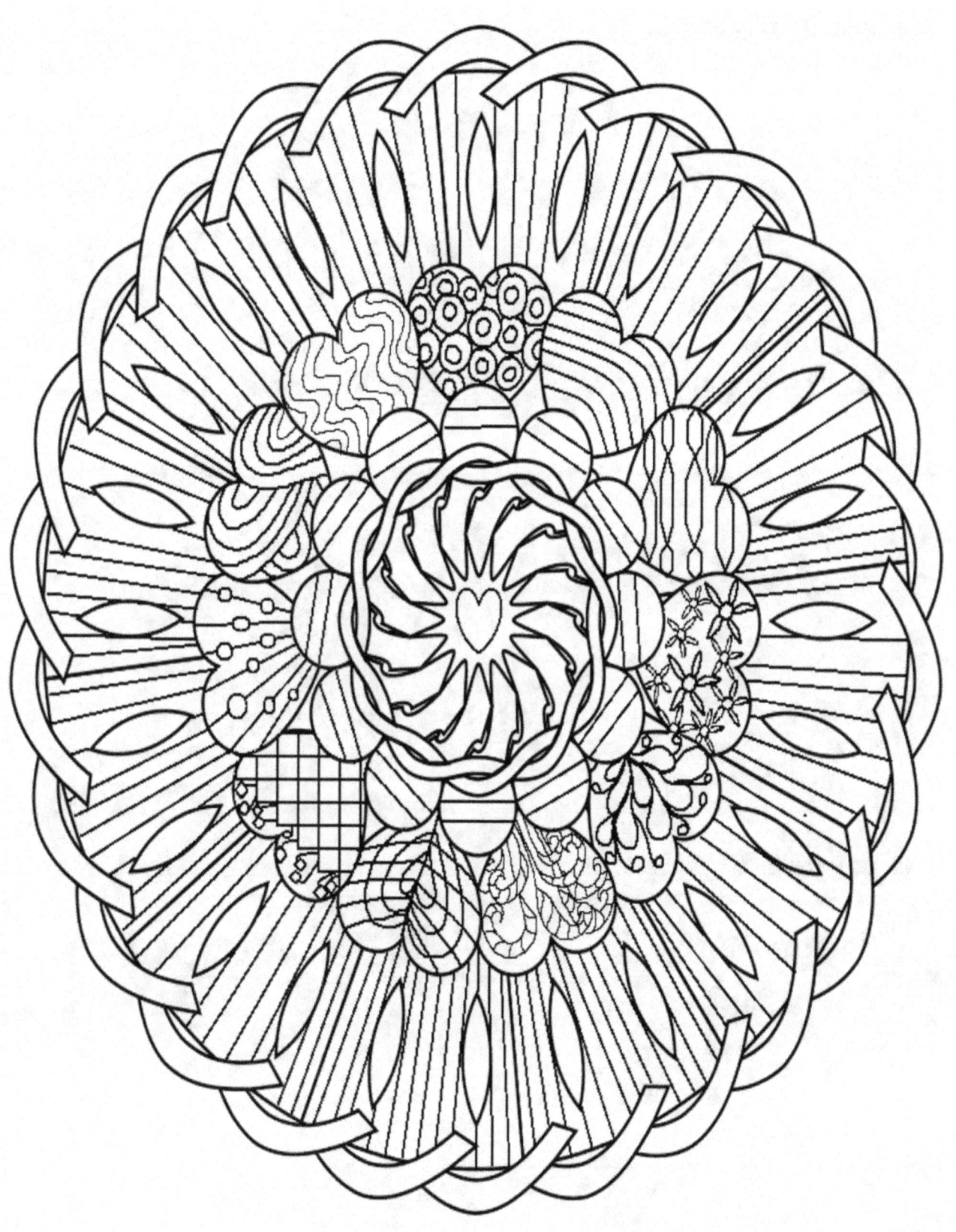

When strife fills the land?

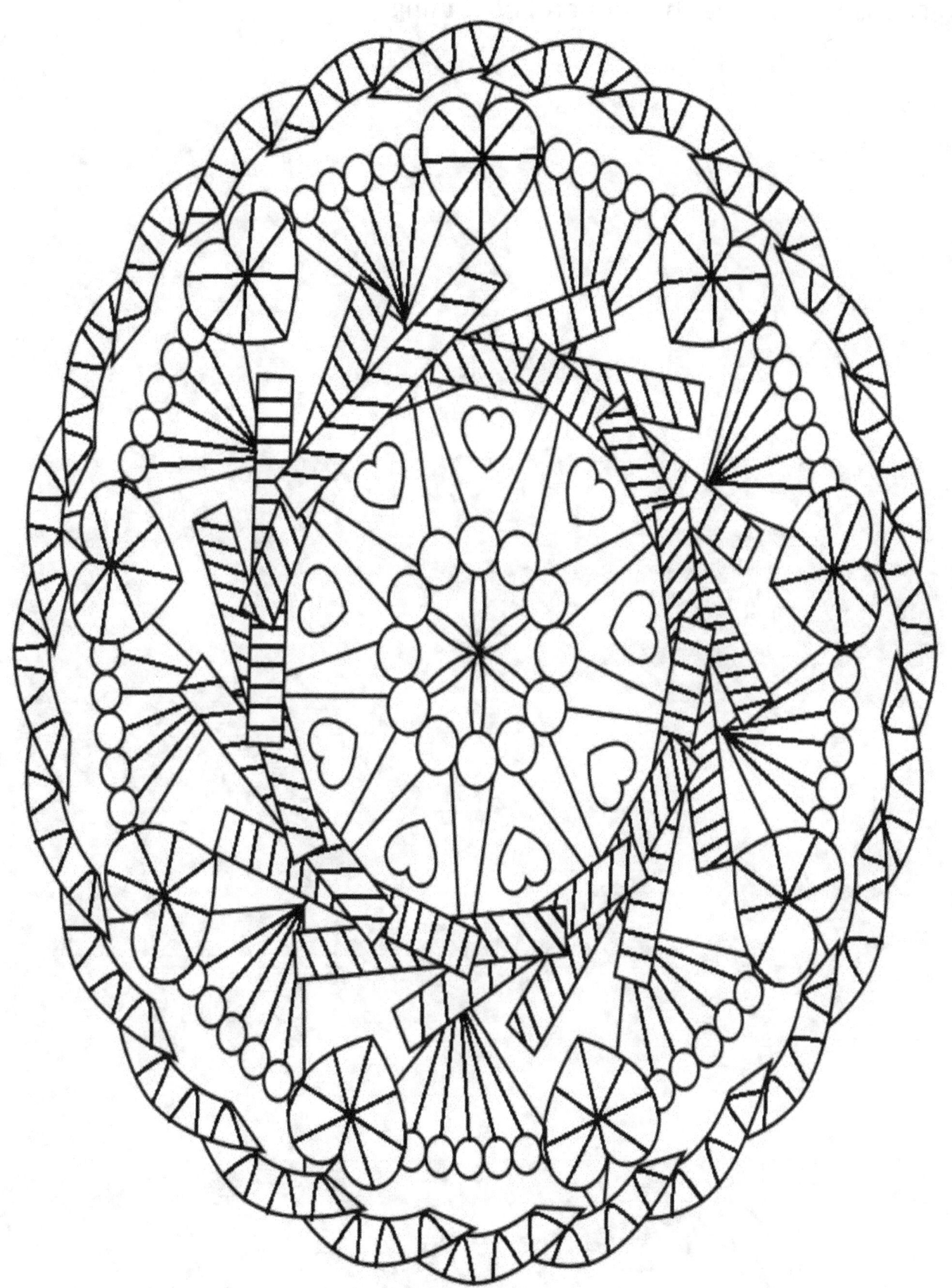

I choose a love that has hopeful beginnings,

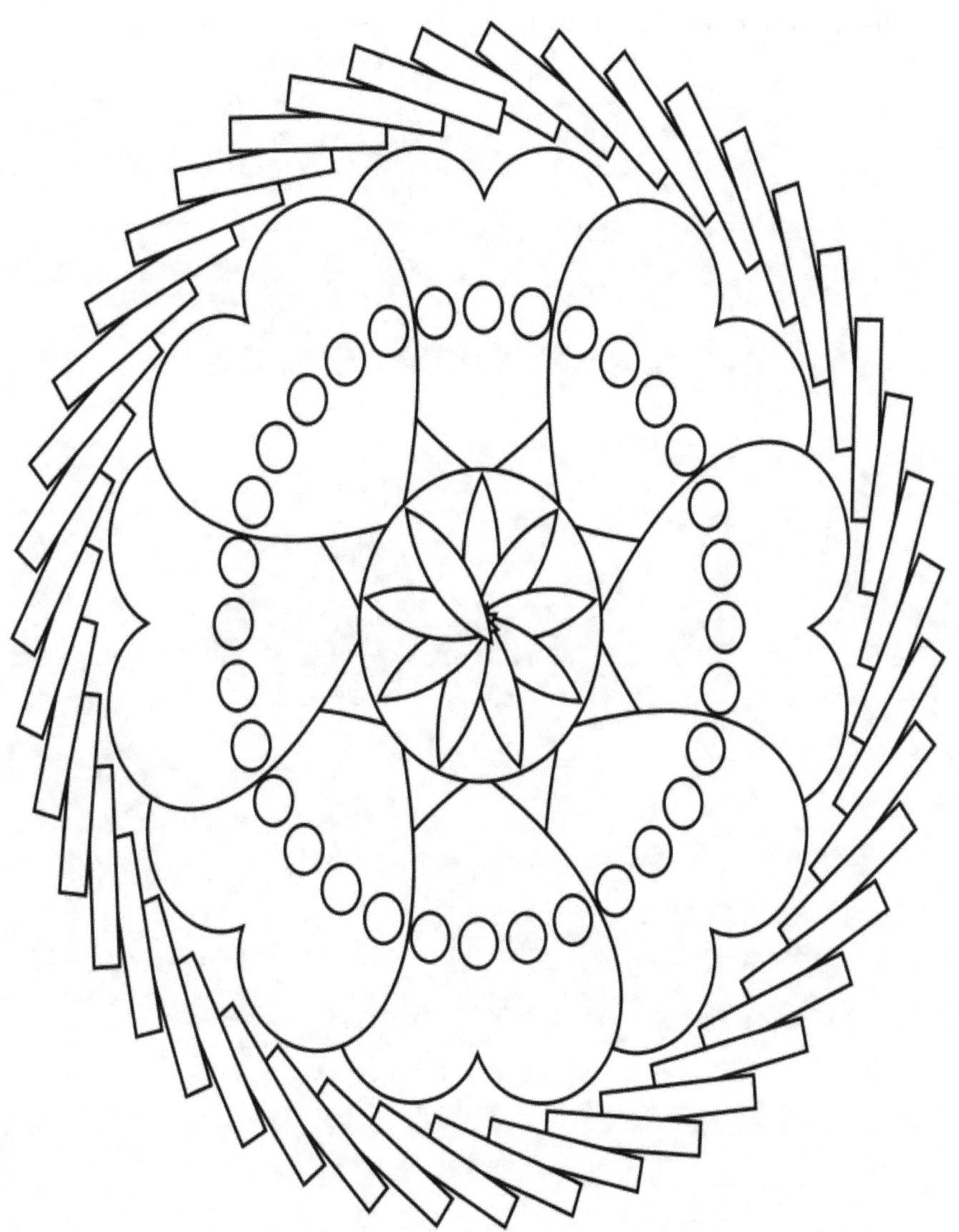

And a faith to see me through,

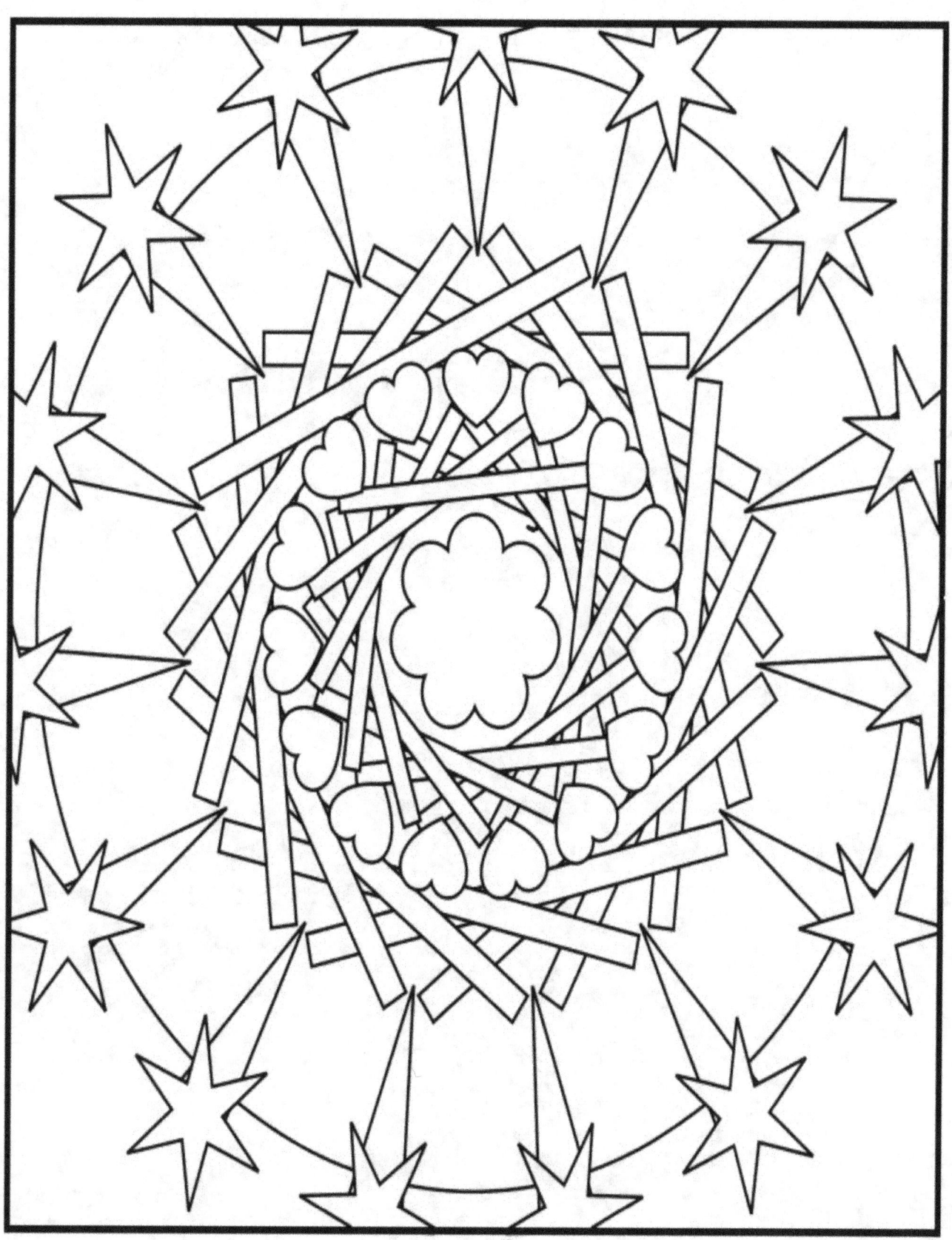

Old things are changed to new,

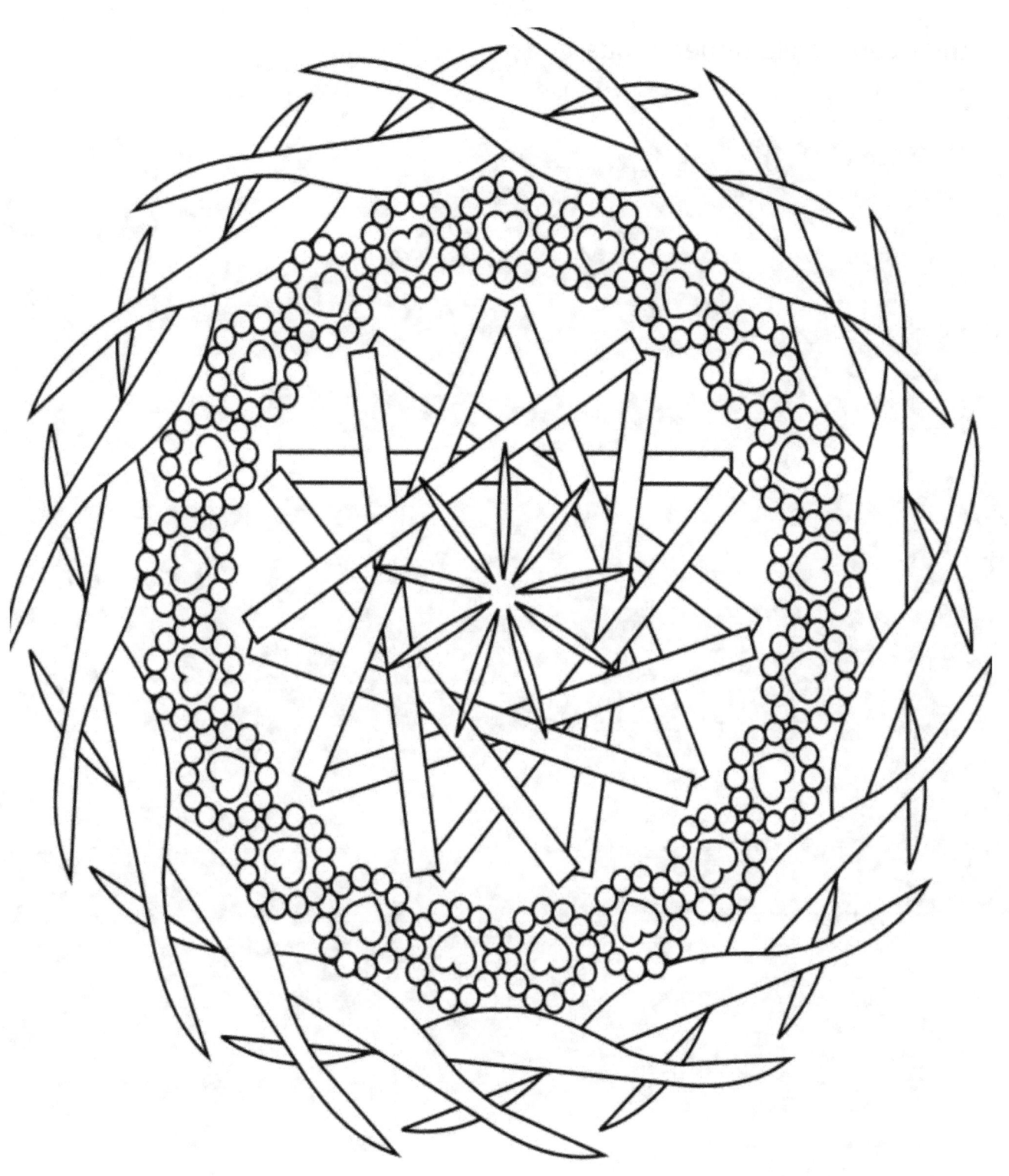

And even a child understands,

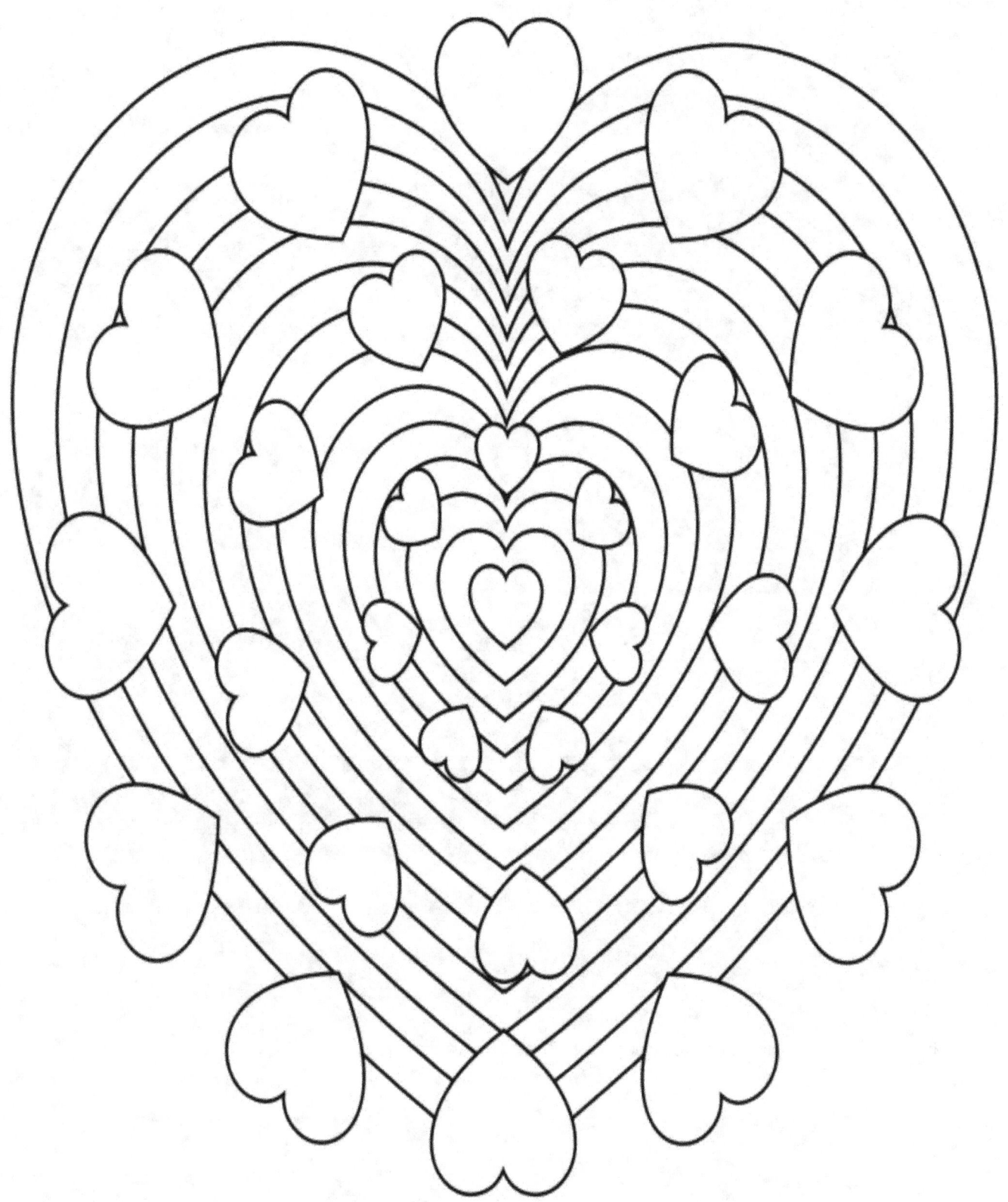

It's a powerful Faith, and Hope, and Love,

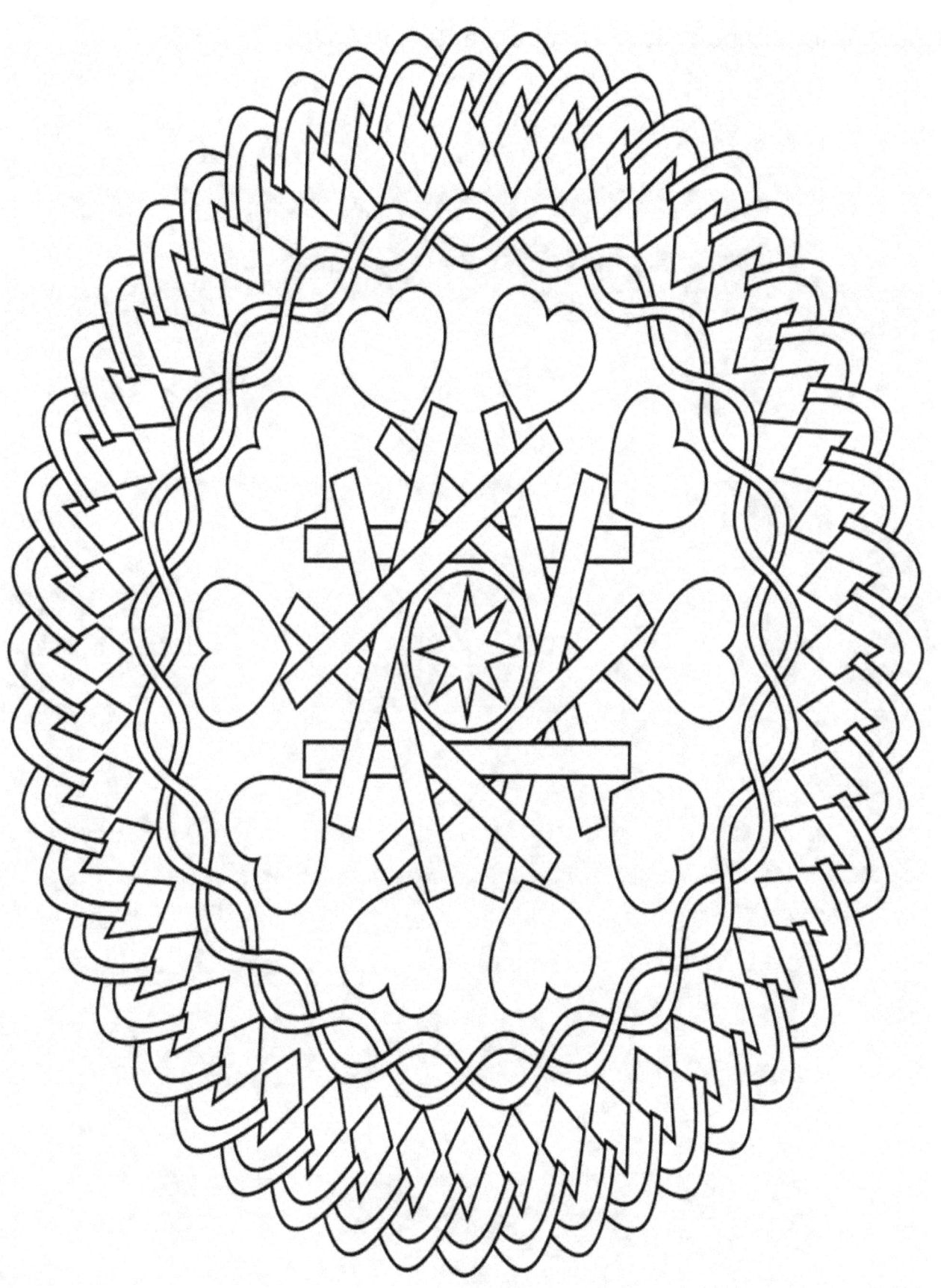

Got to understand that Faith, and Hope, and Love,

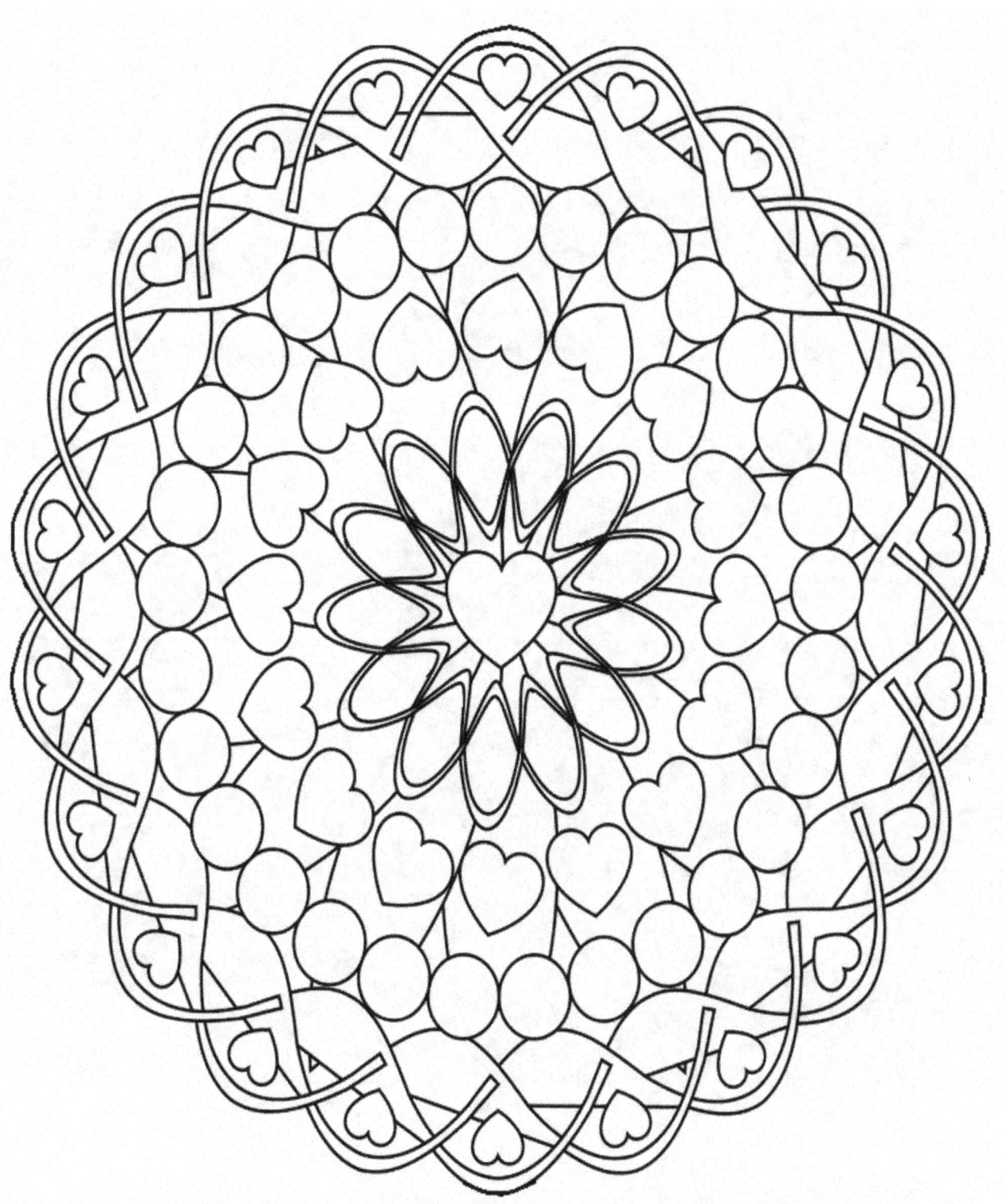

Got to focus on that Faith, and Hope and Love,

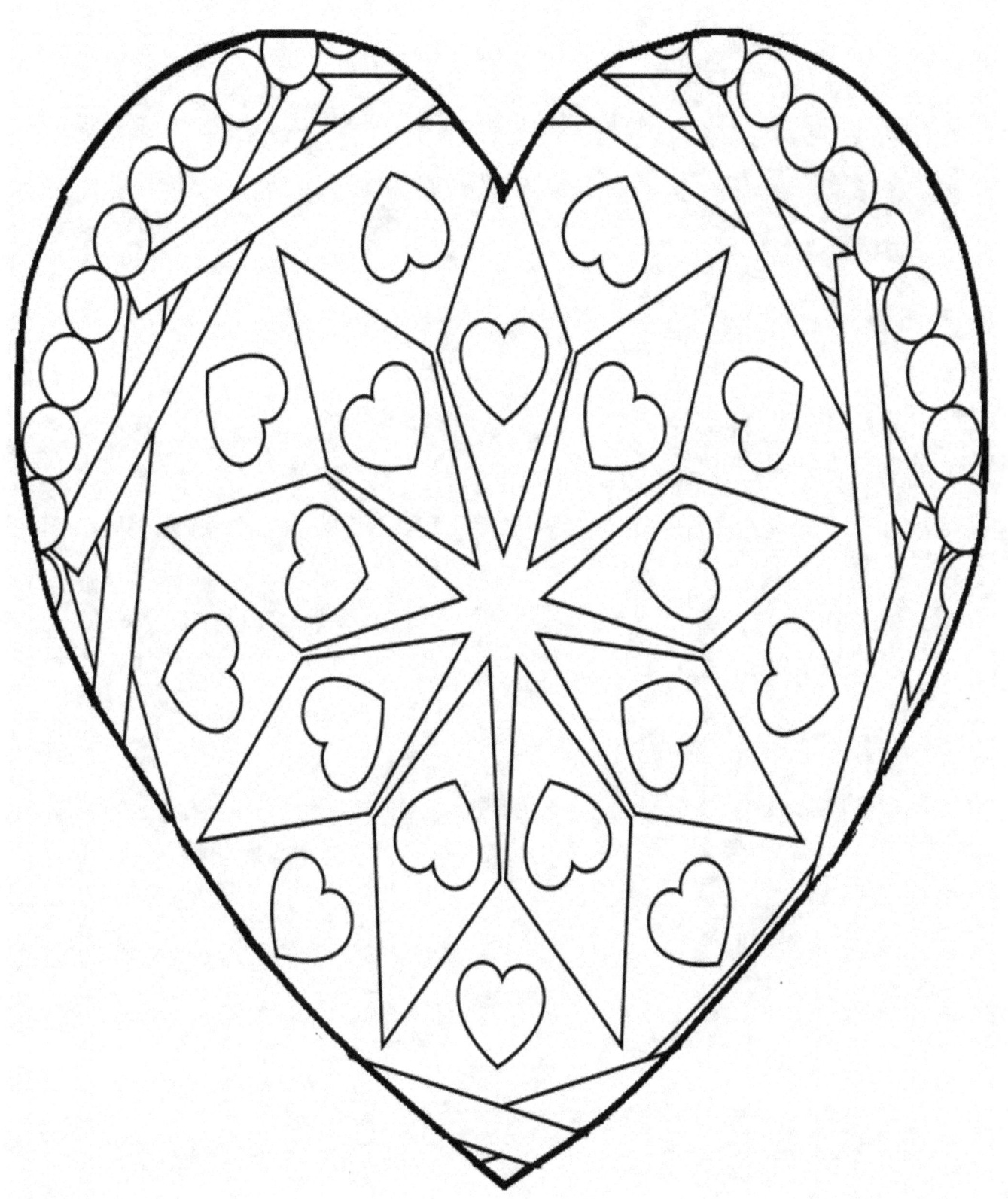

But the greatest is Love

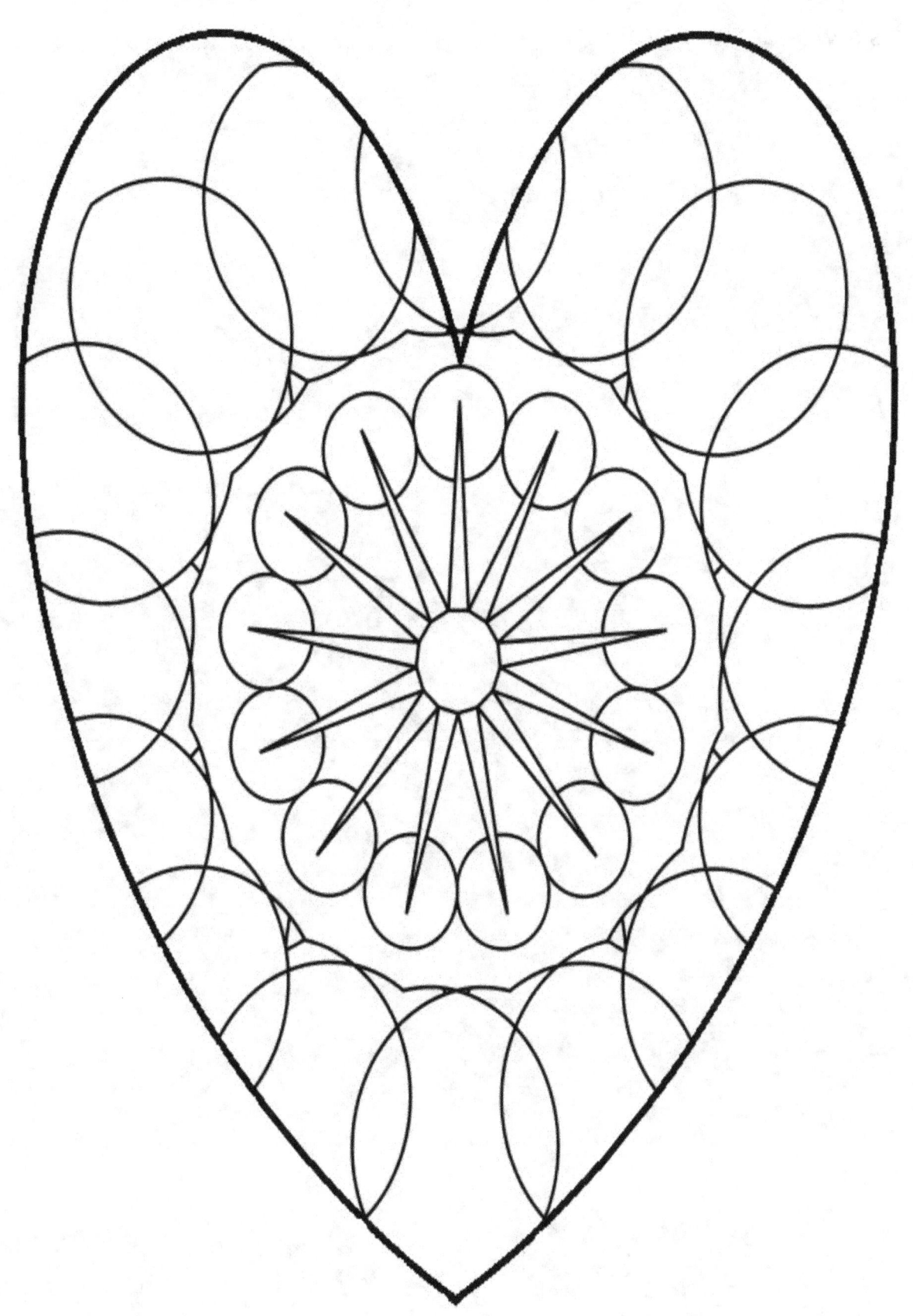

It's a wonderful Love!

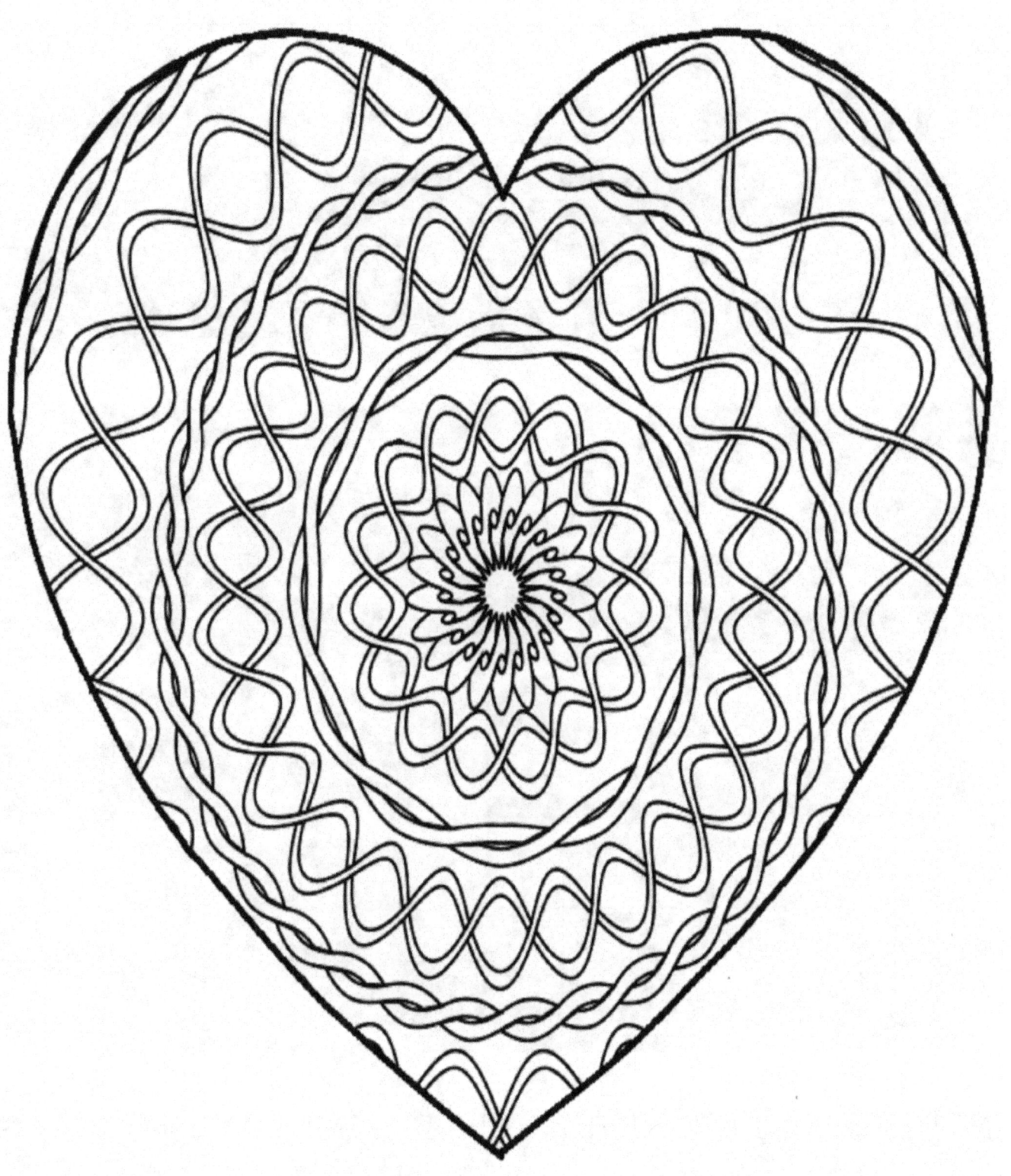

This Love is kind,

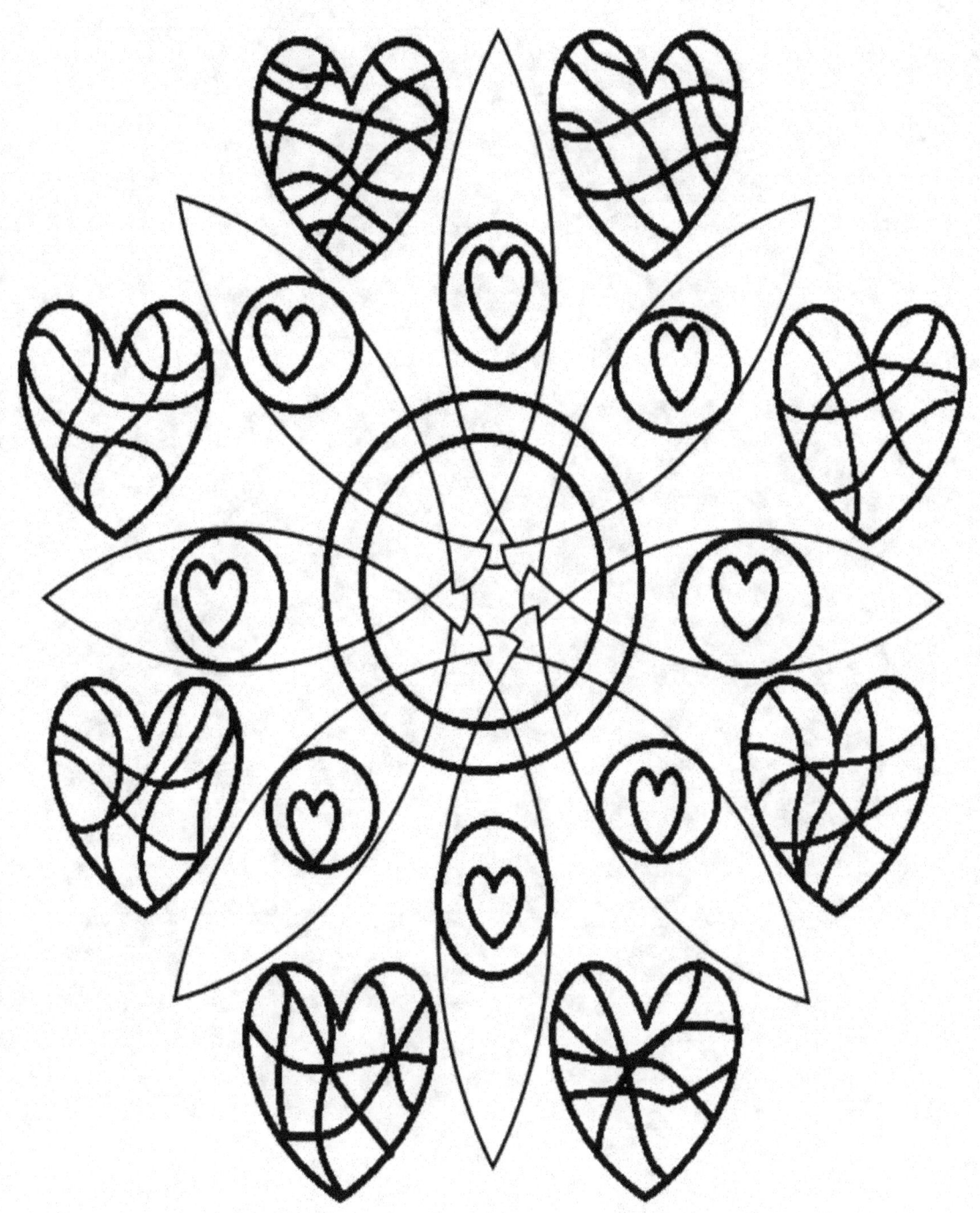

It does not behave rudely.

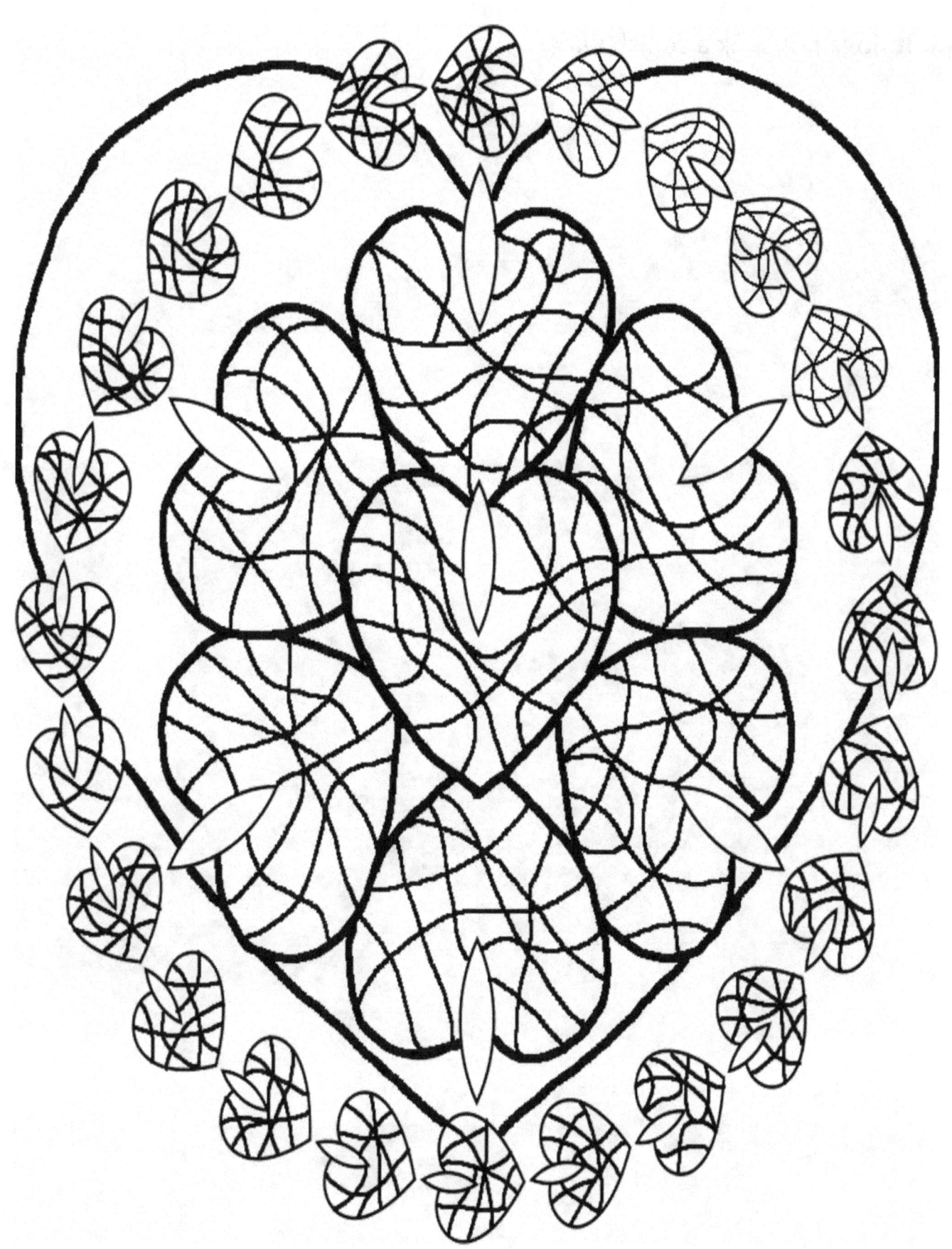

It does not seek a selfish way.

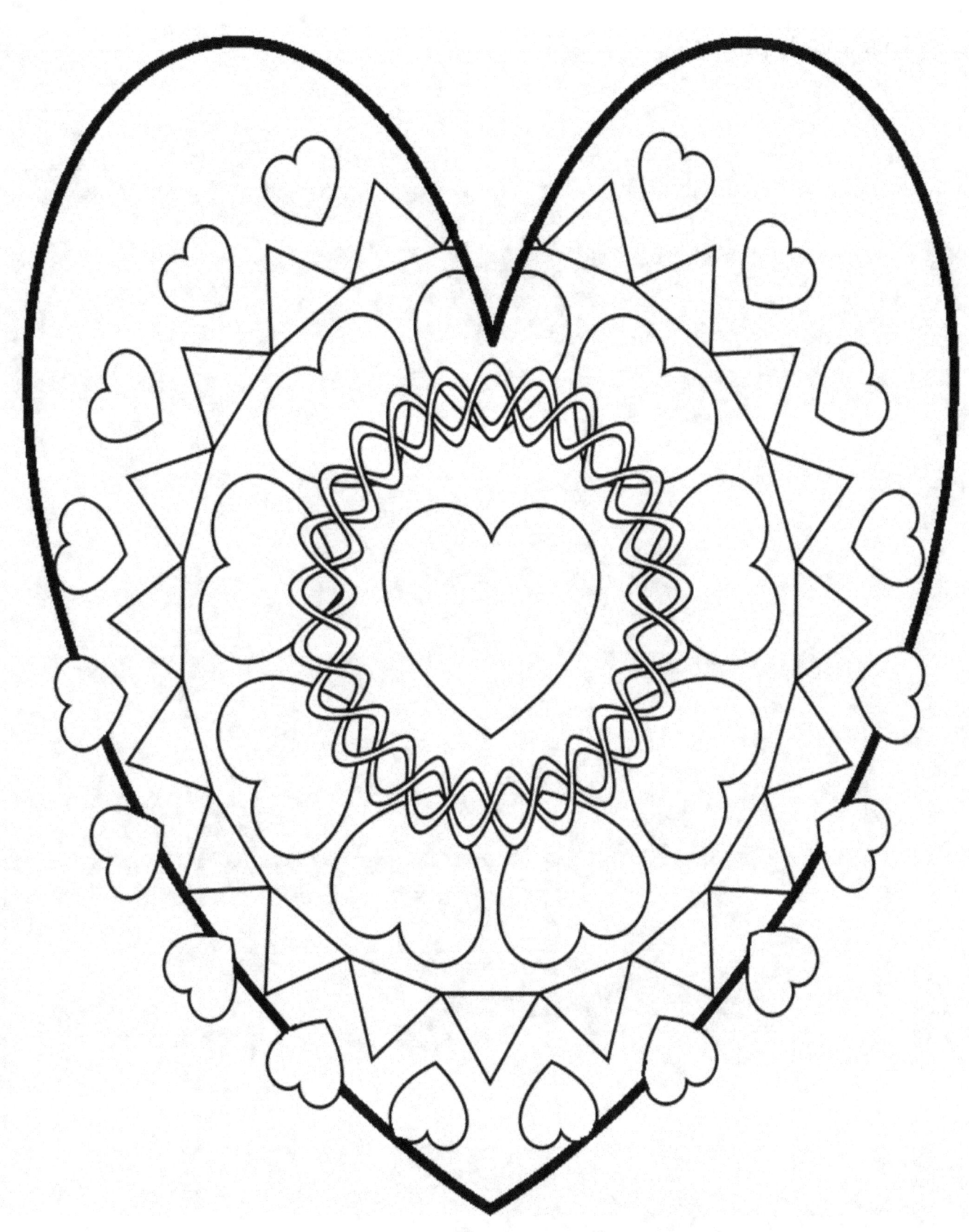

This love is patient,

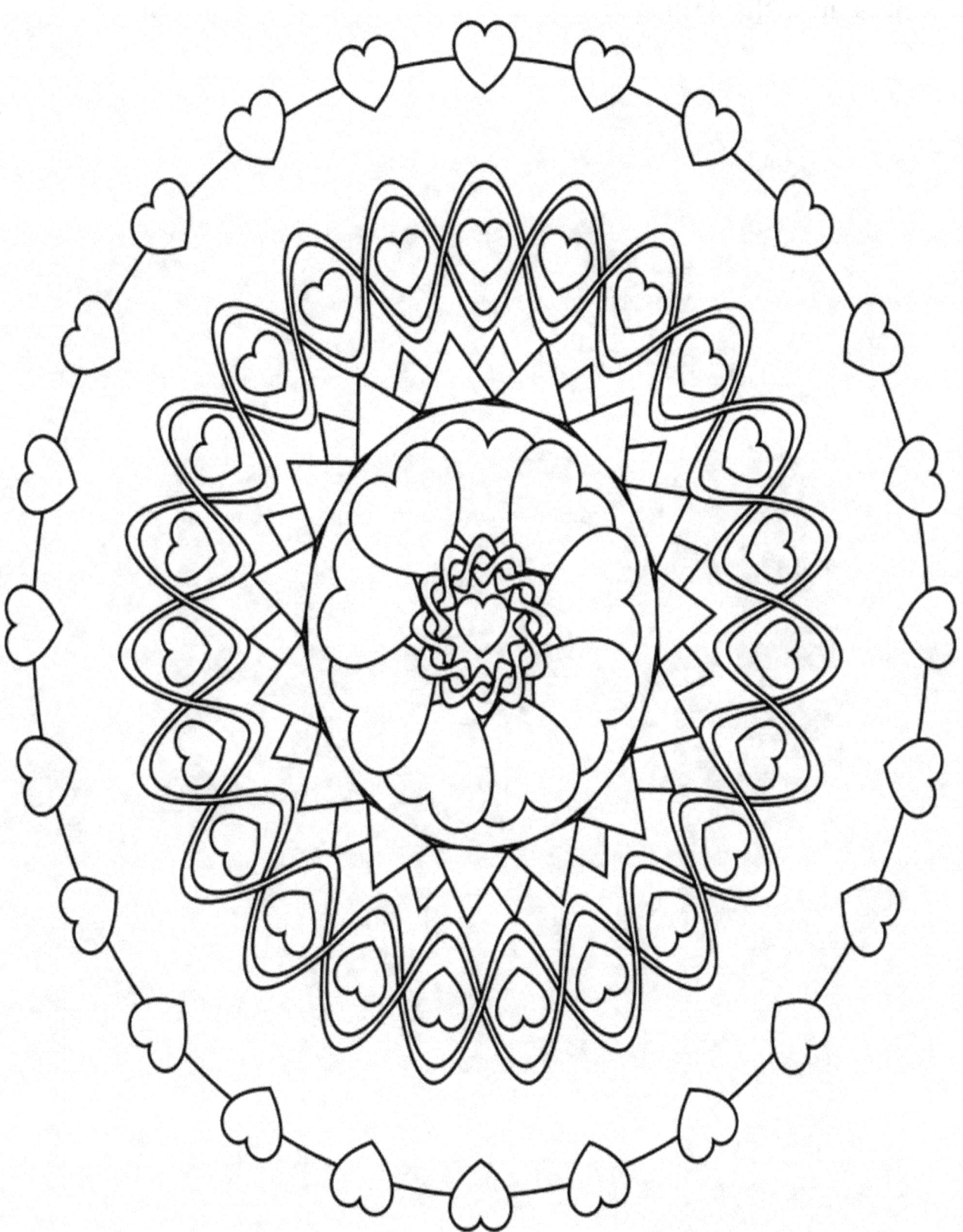

It puts up with all things.

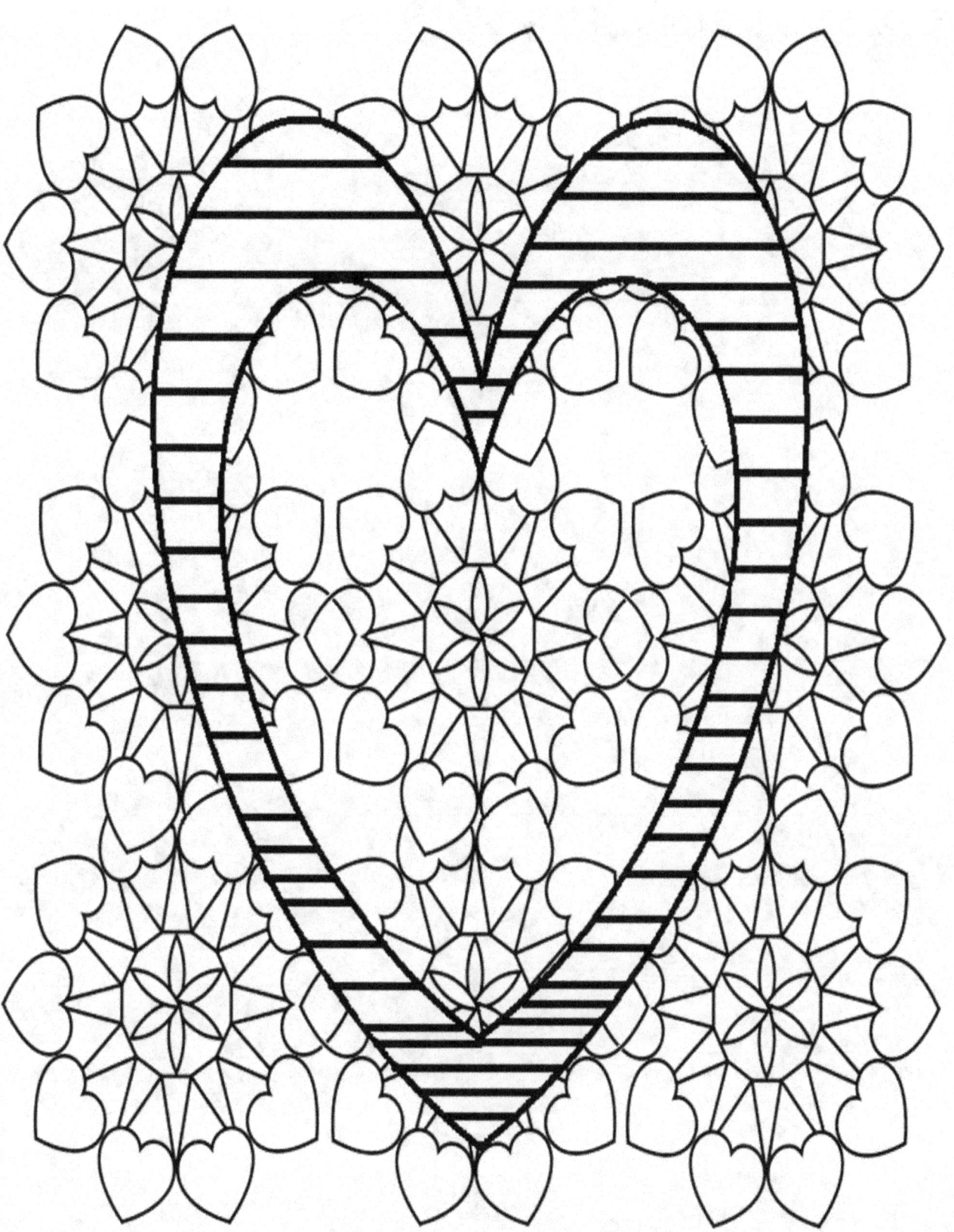

It's wise with words it has to say.

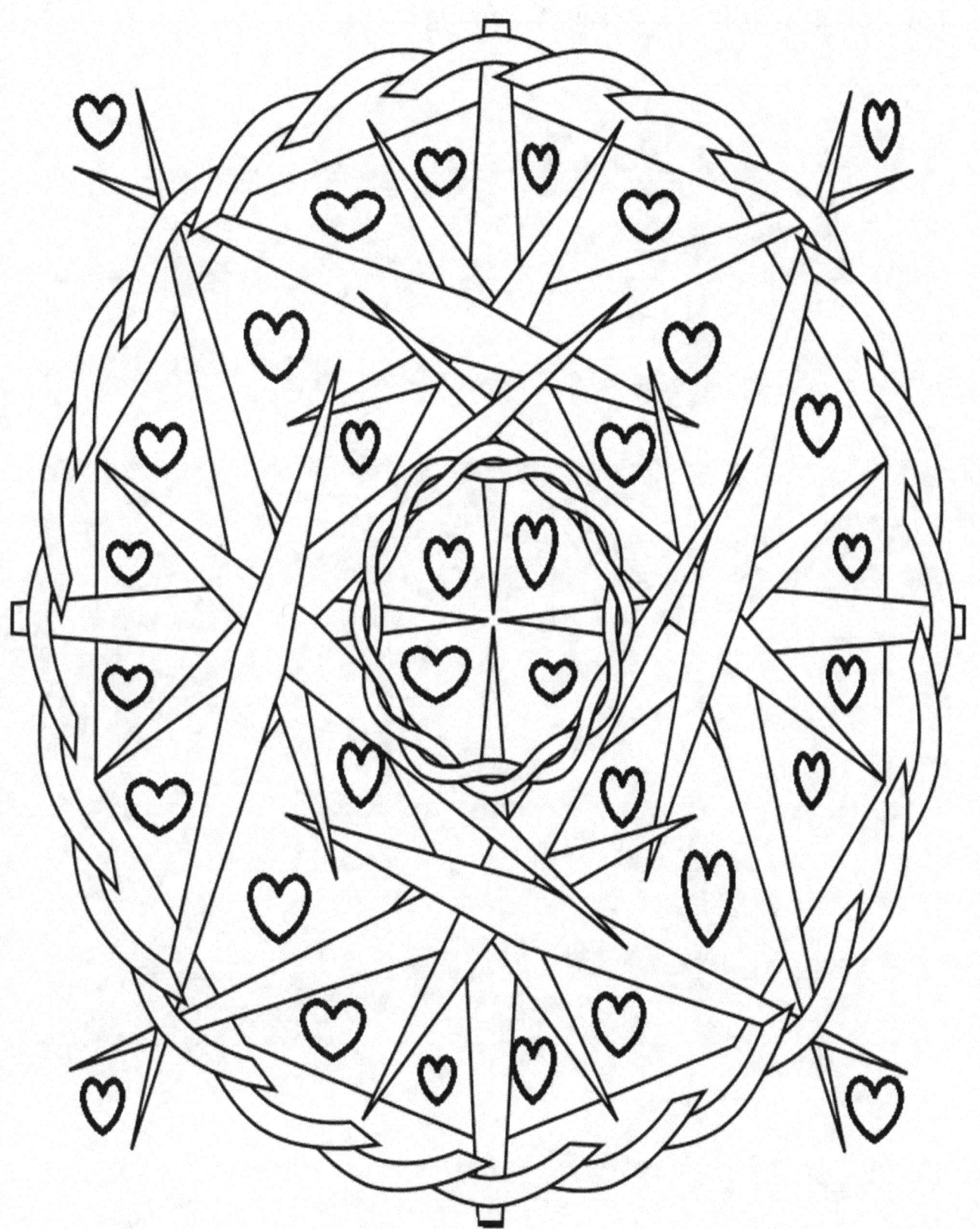

What does it profit if love is not winning?

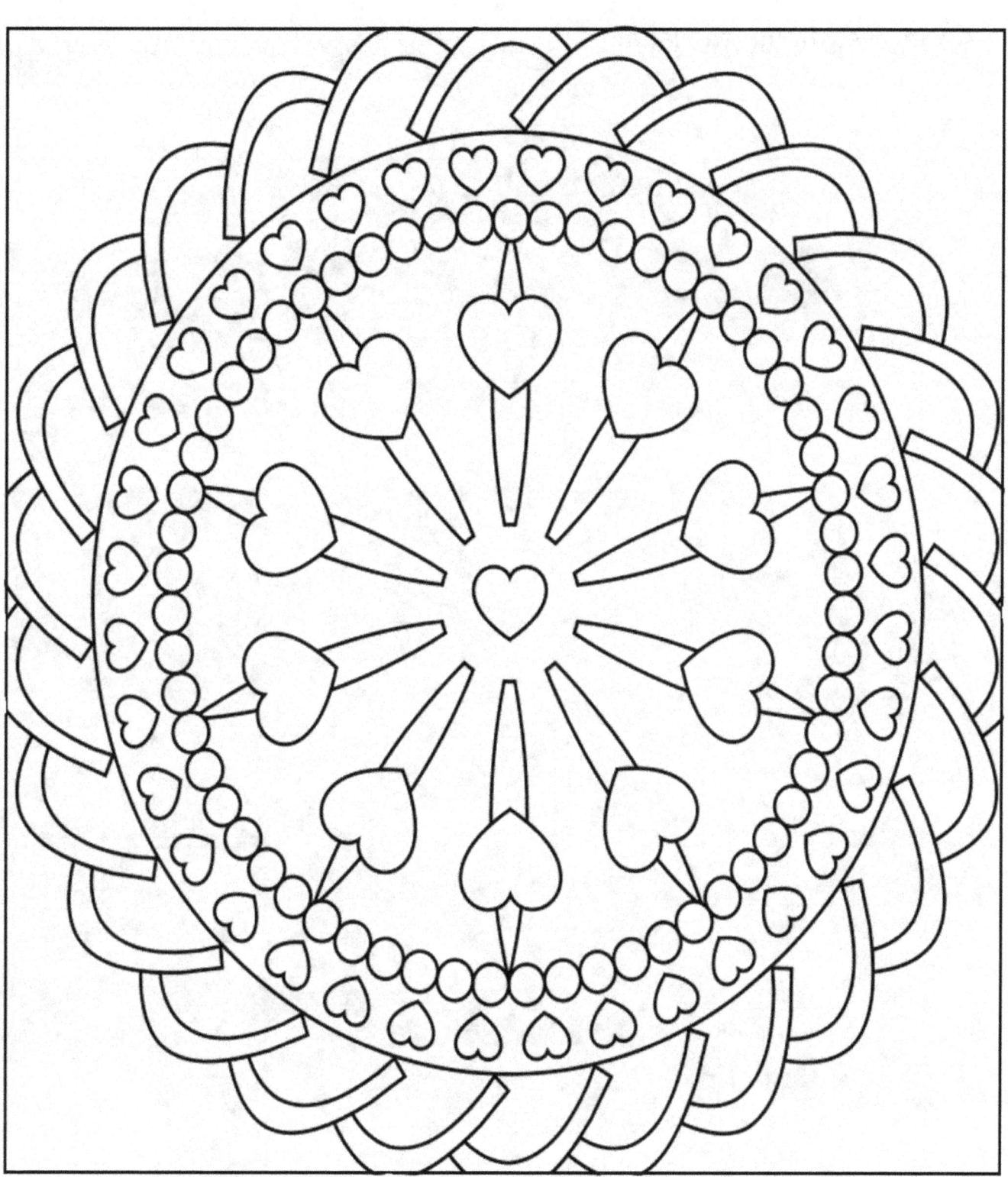

When strife fills the land.

I choose a love that has hopeful beginnings.

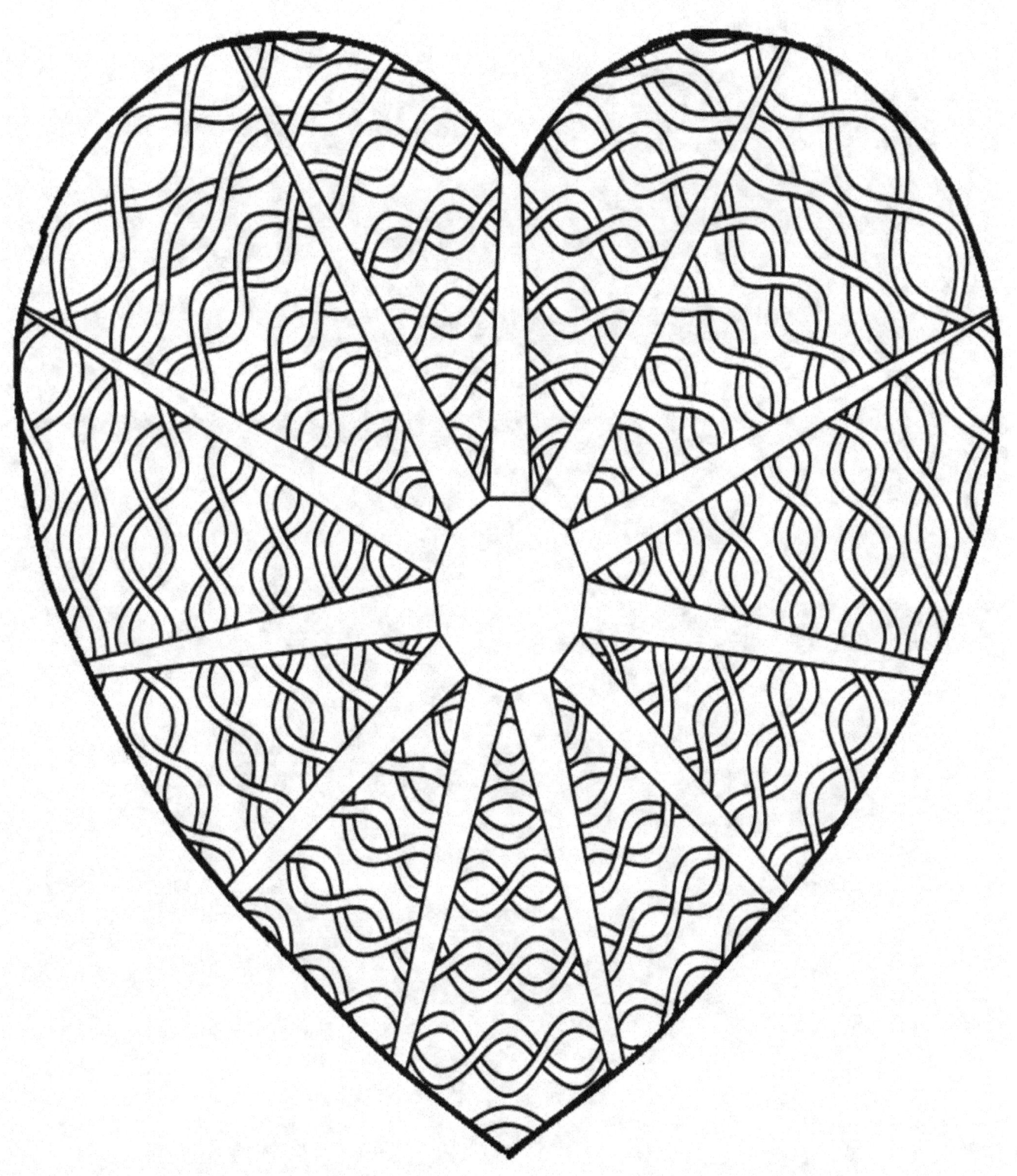

And a faith that sees me through

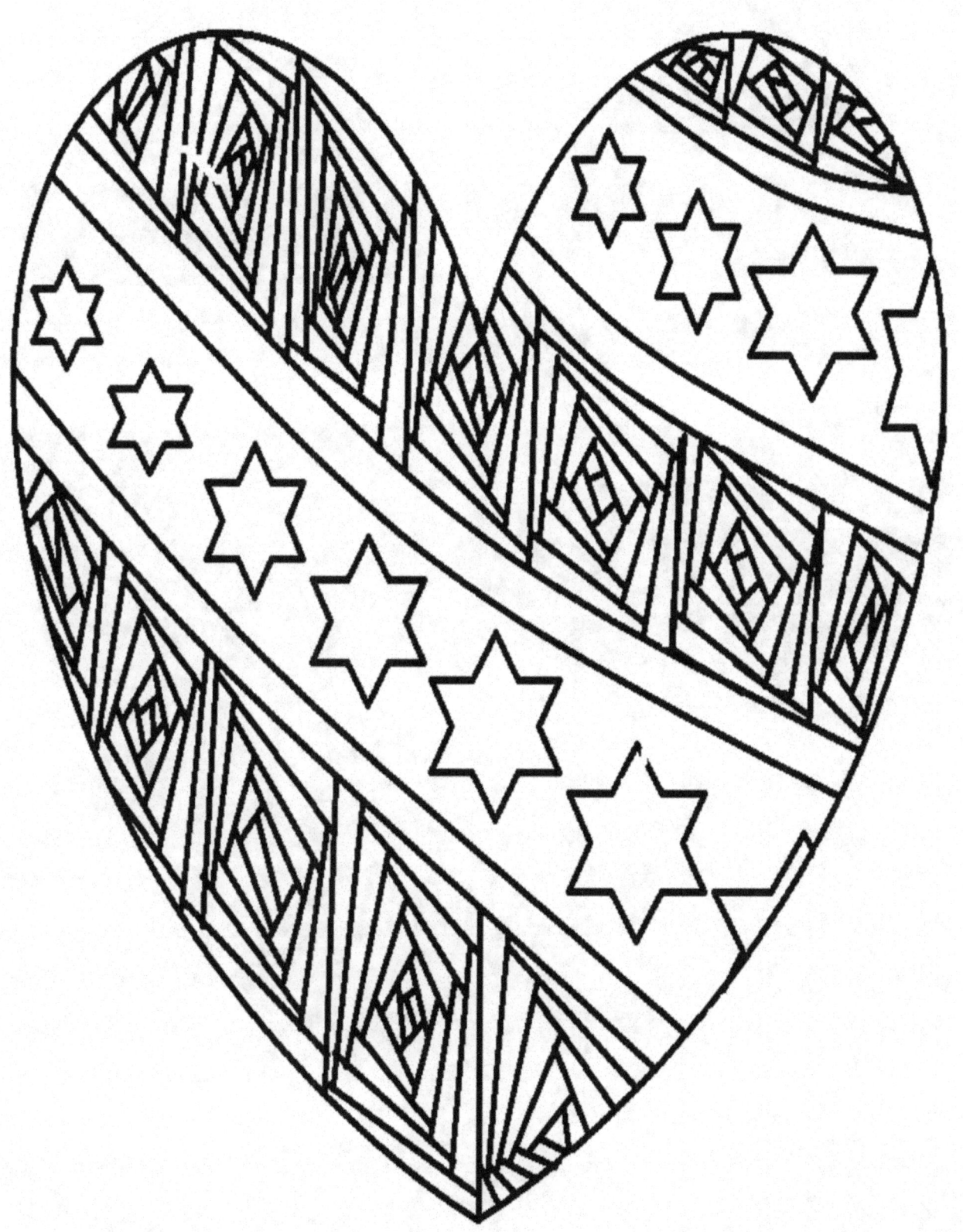

Old things are changed to new,

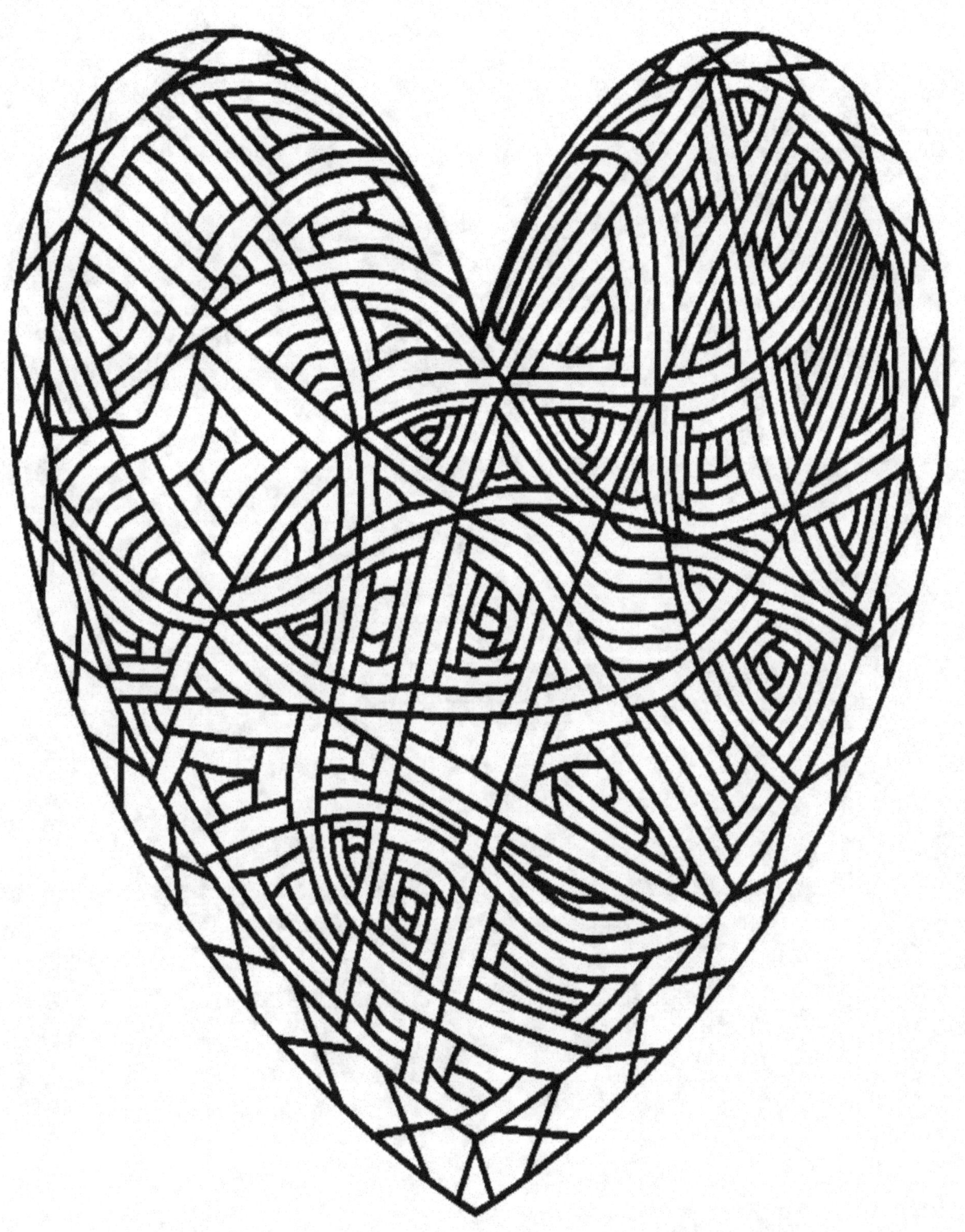

And even a child understands

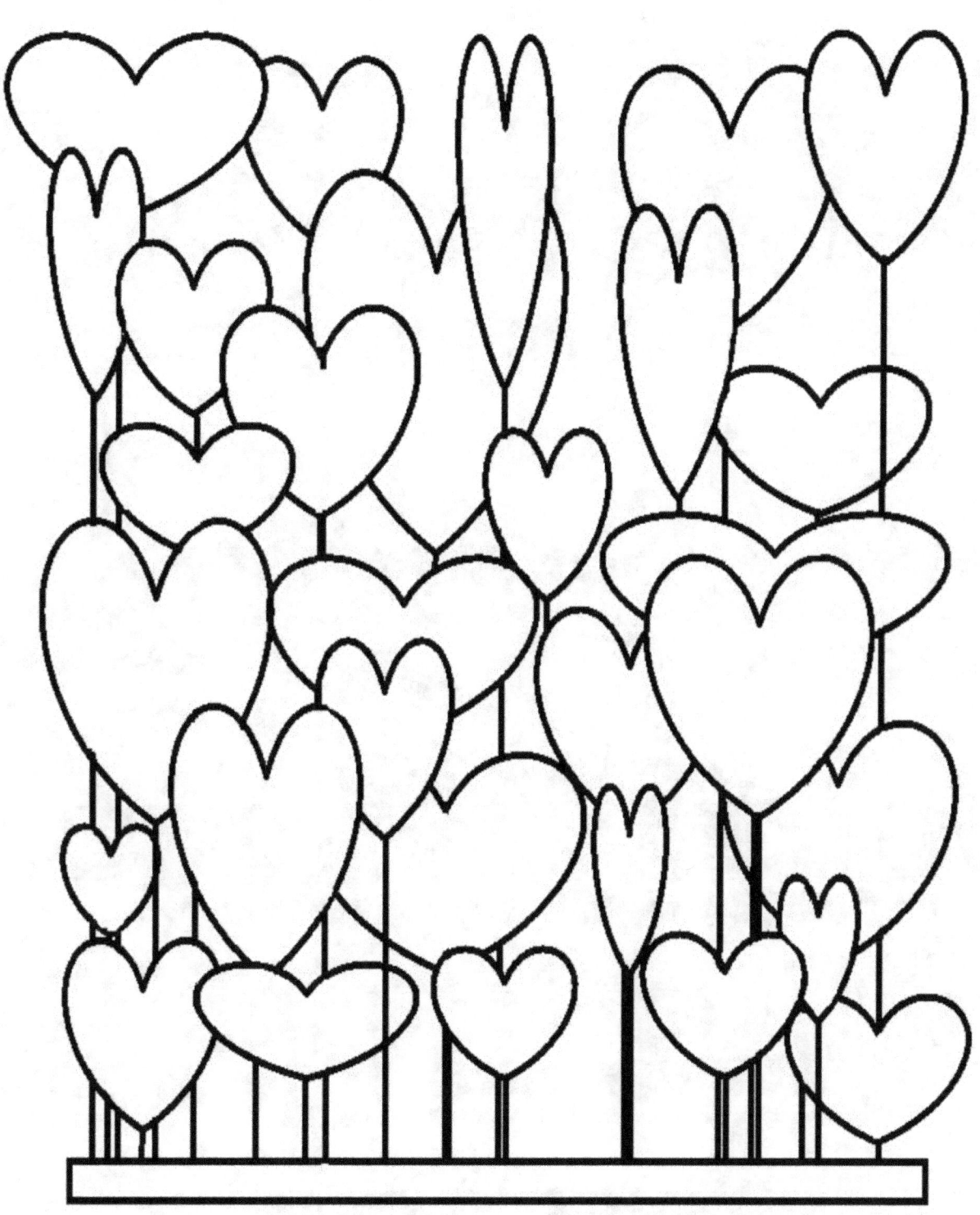

It's a powerful faith and hope and love.

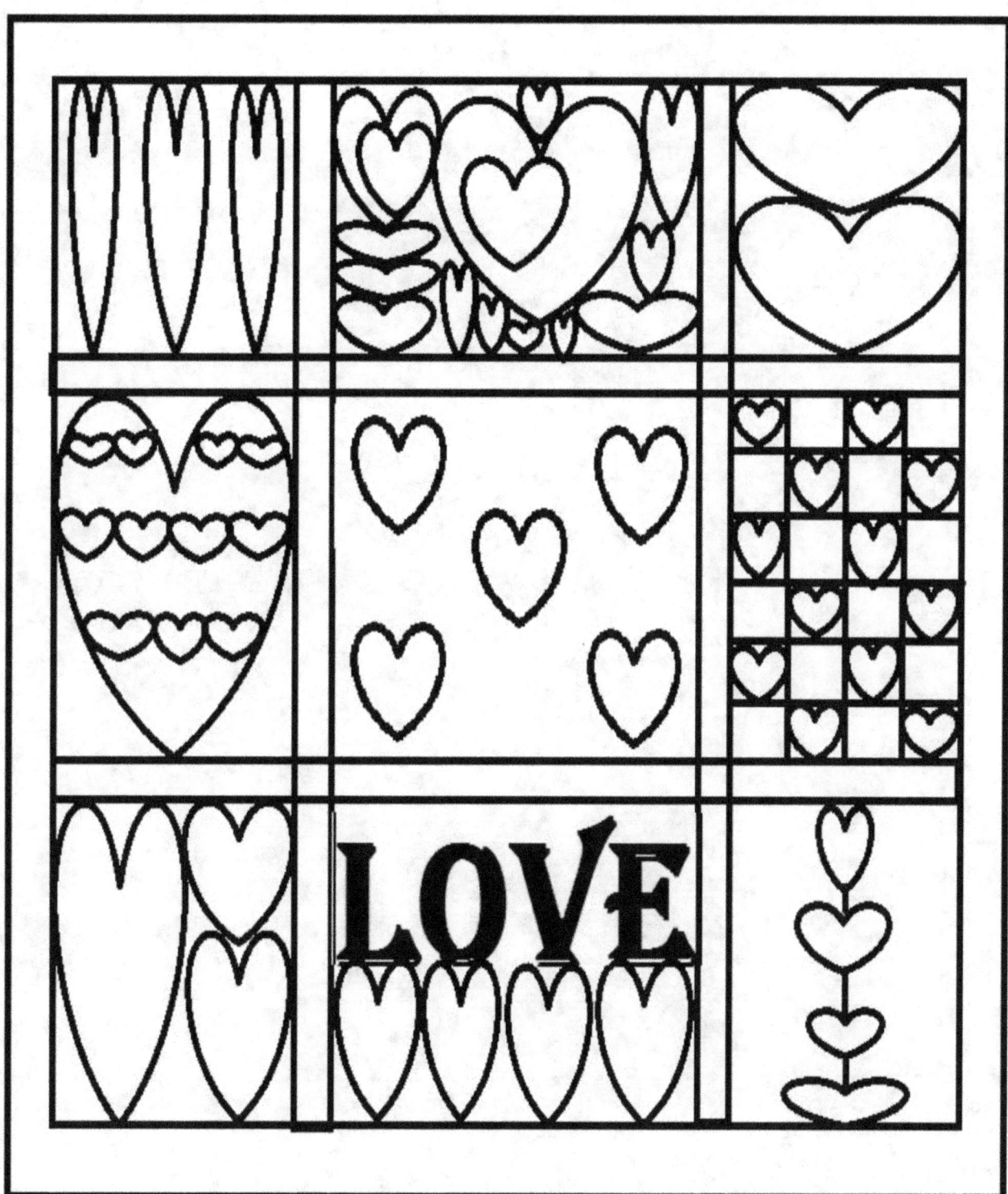

Got to understand that faith and hope and love.

Got to focus on that faith and hope on love.

But the greatest is love,

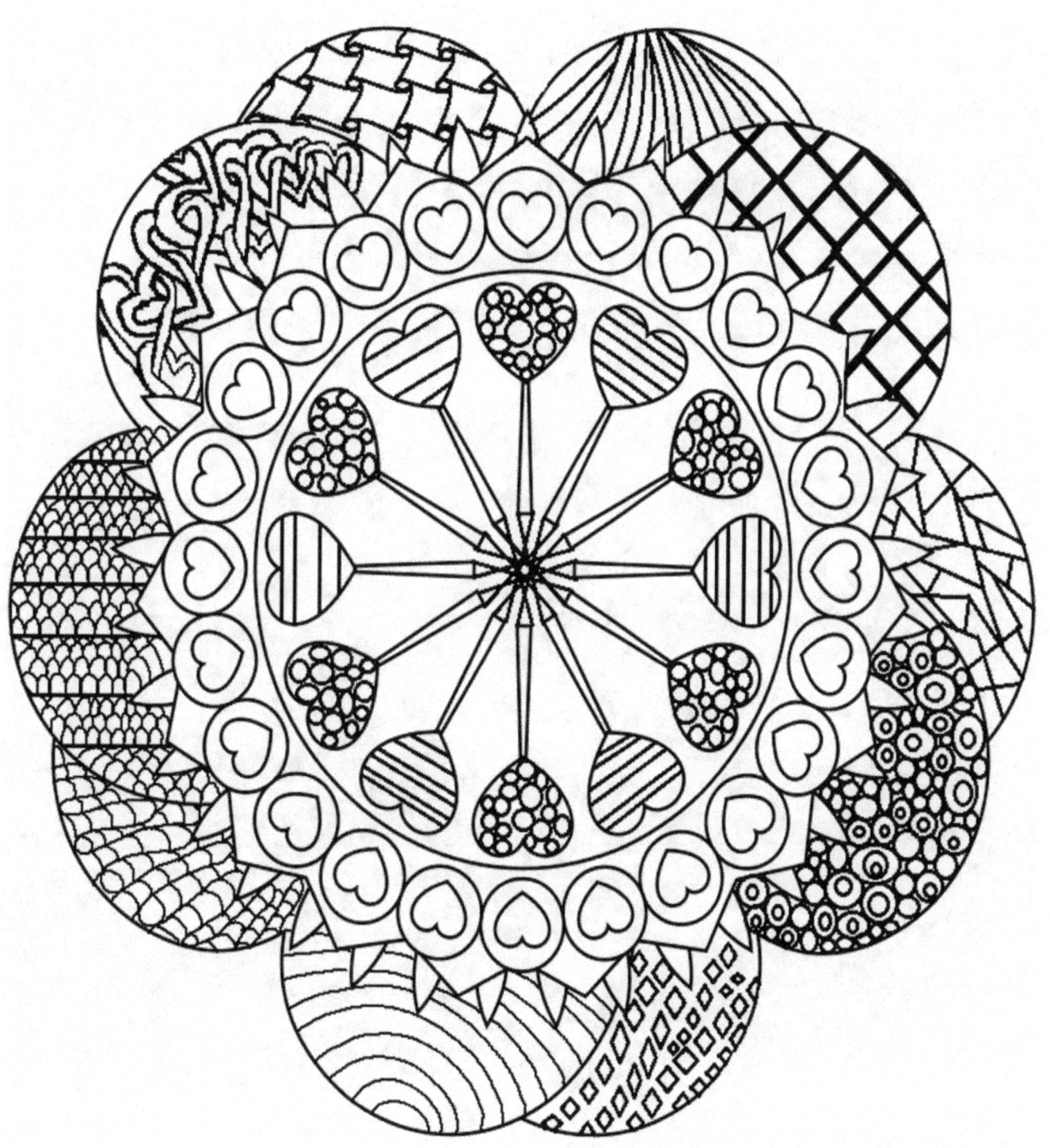

It's wonderful love.

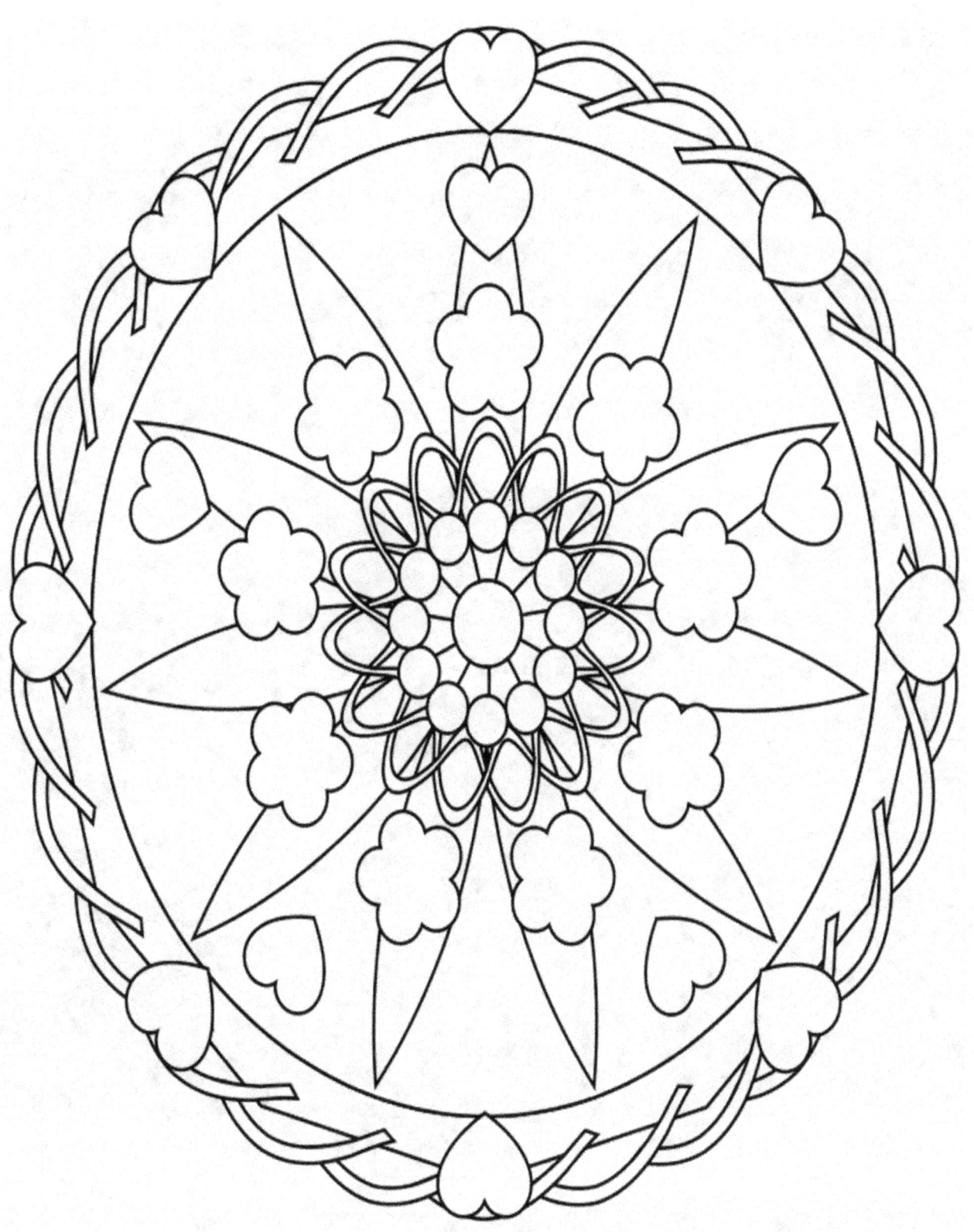

Oh there will be a day

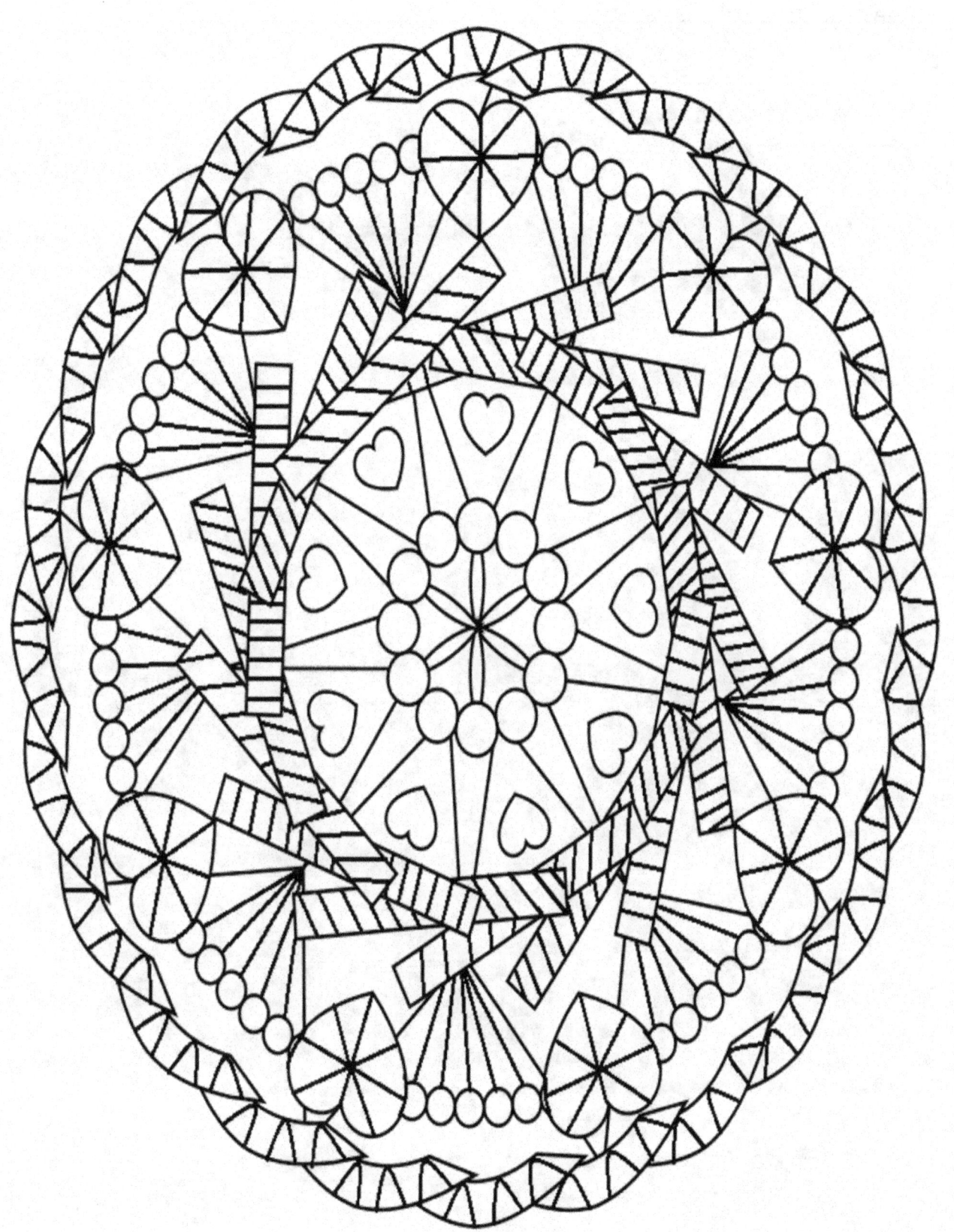

Hope and faith will pass away,

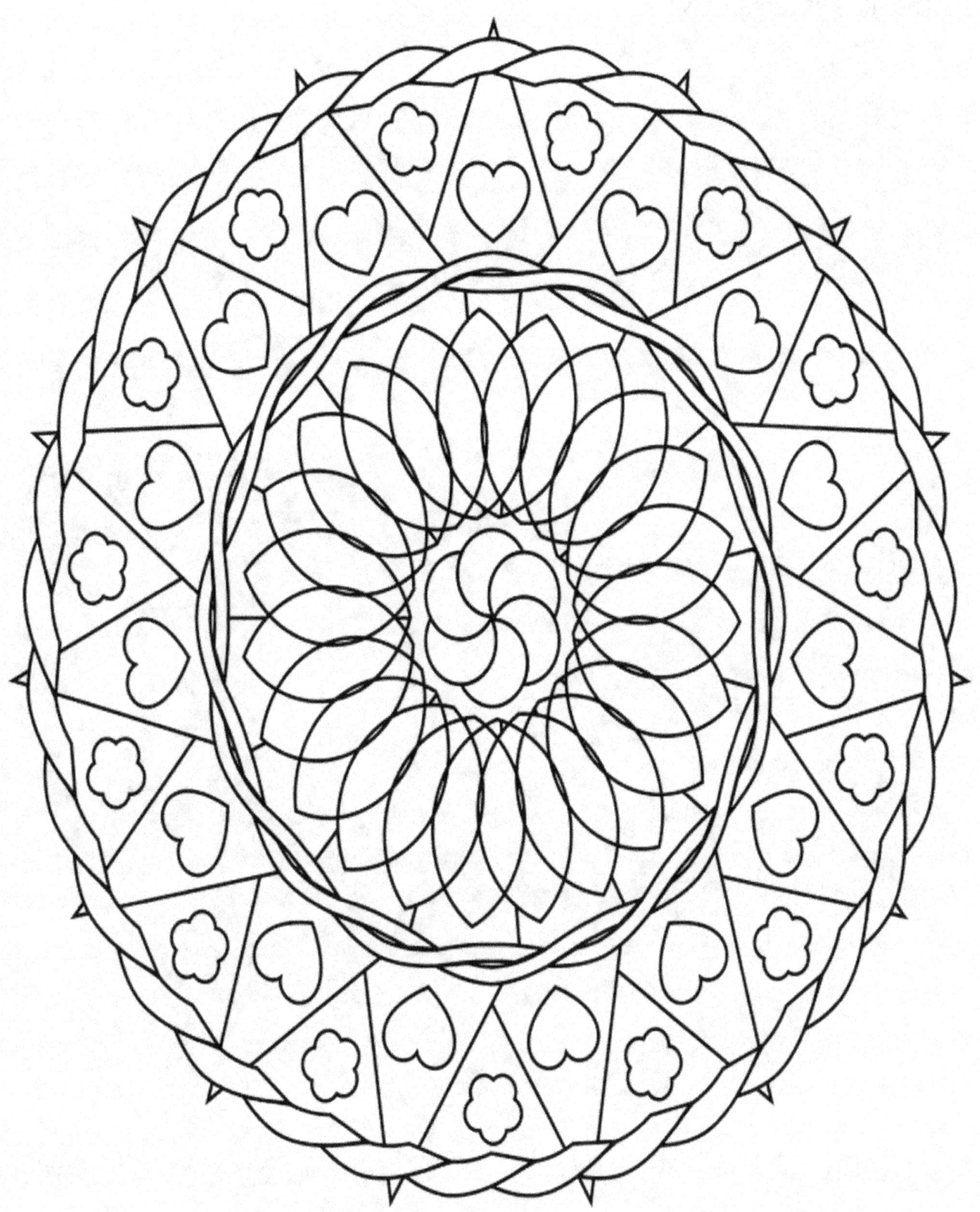

And all that remains is love.

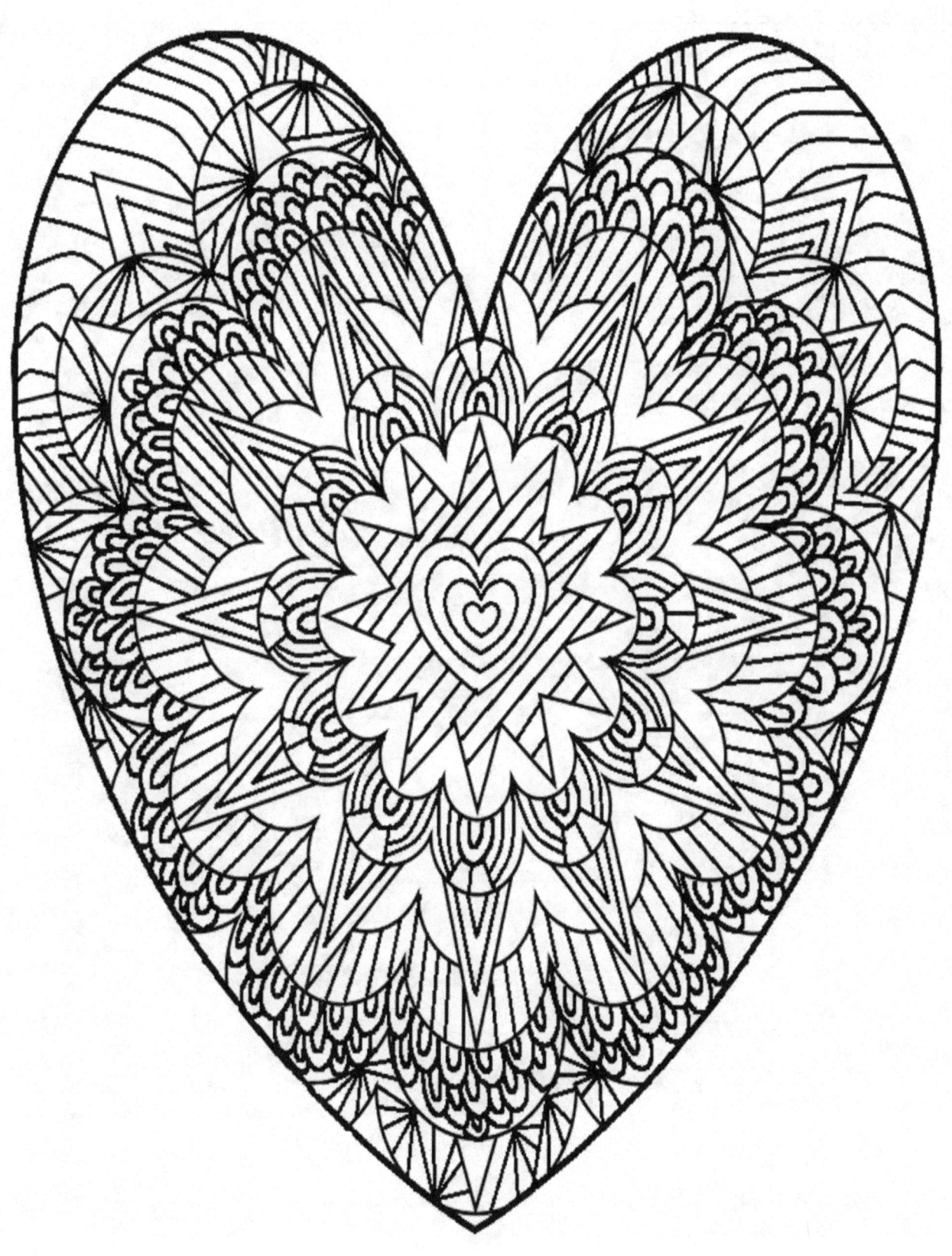

I'll see Jesus face to face

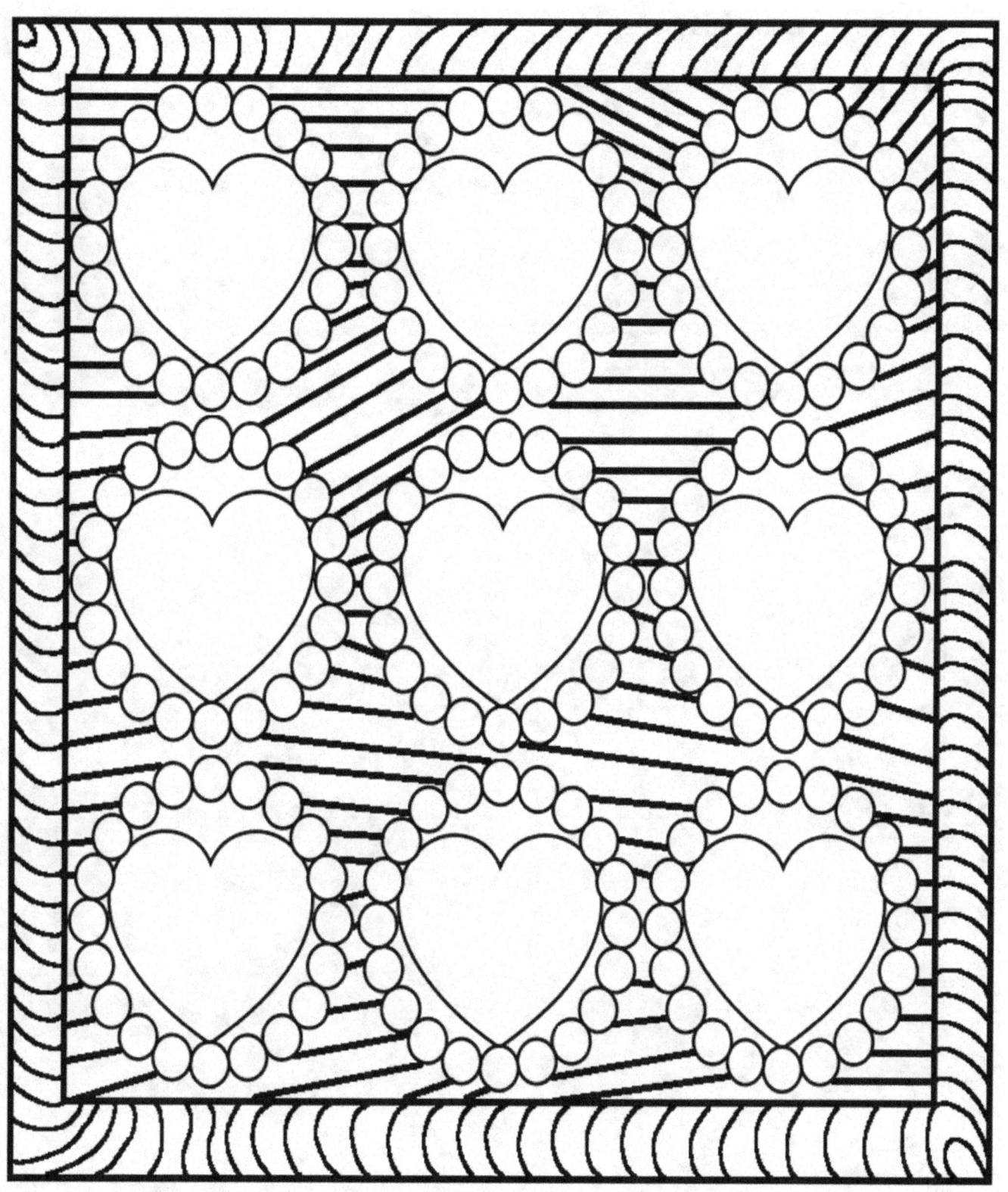

Relish in His wondrous grace,

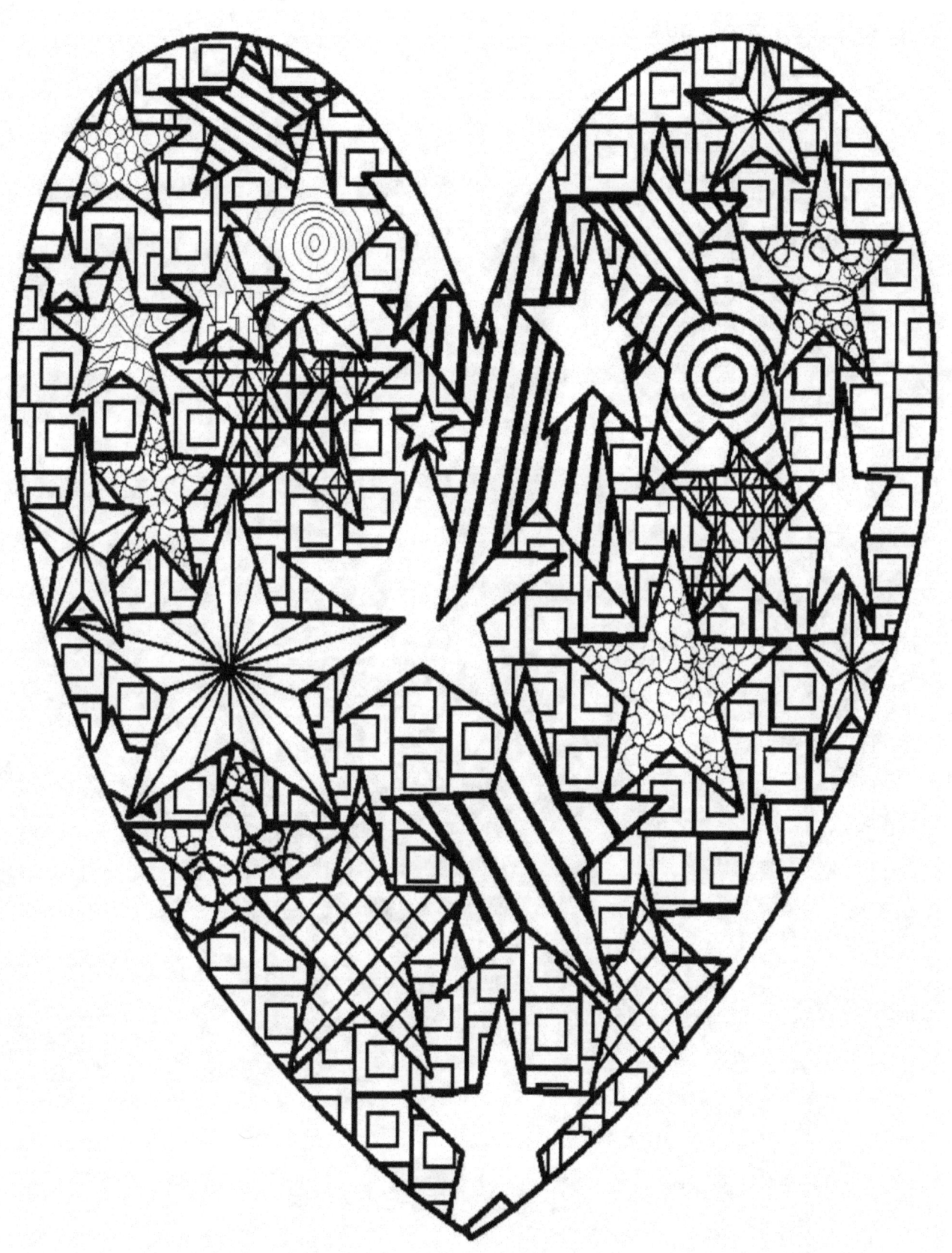

The perfect one from above!

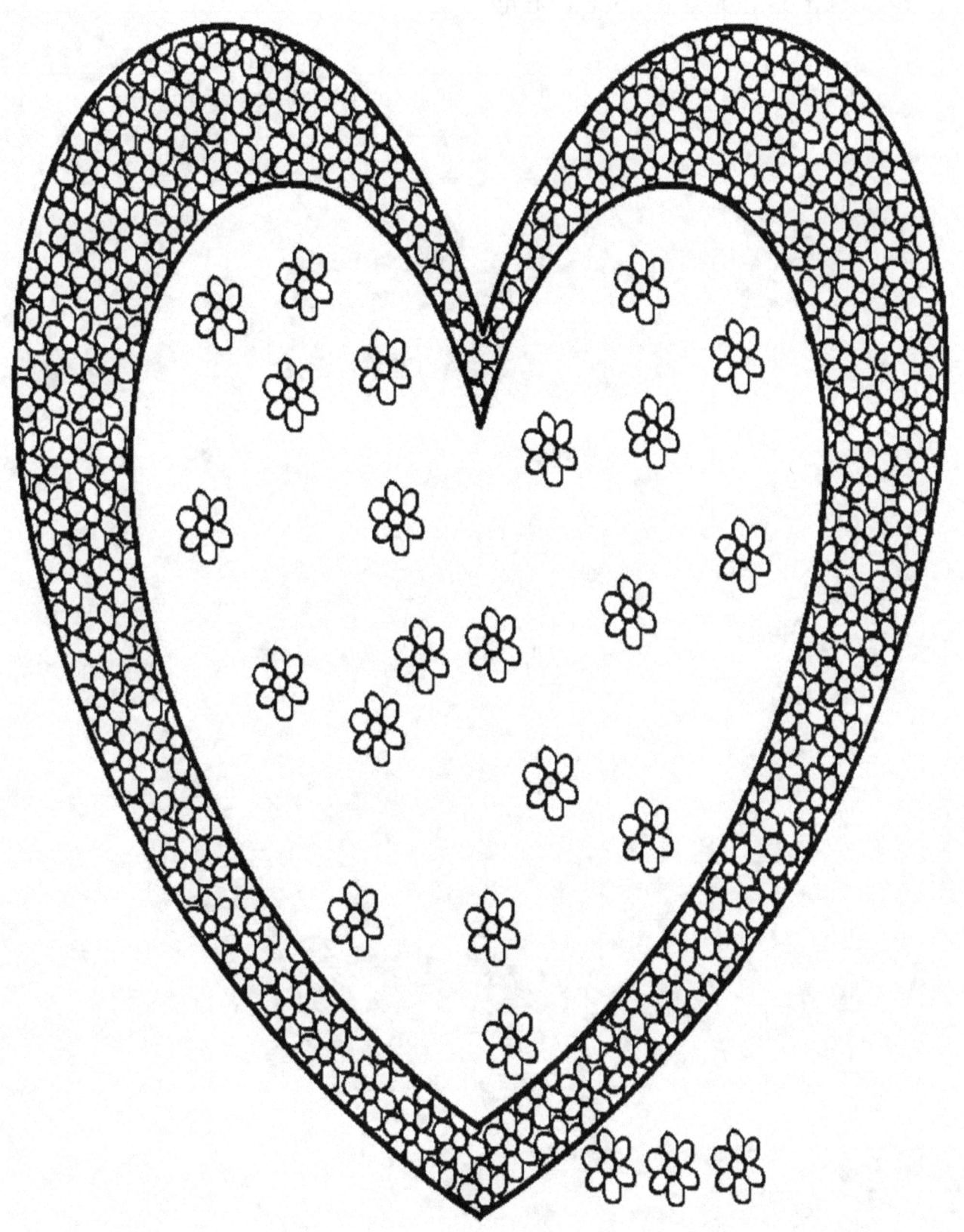

What does it profit if love is not winning?

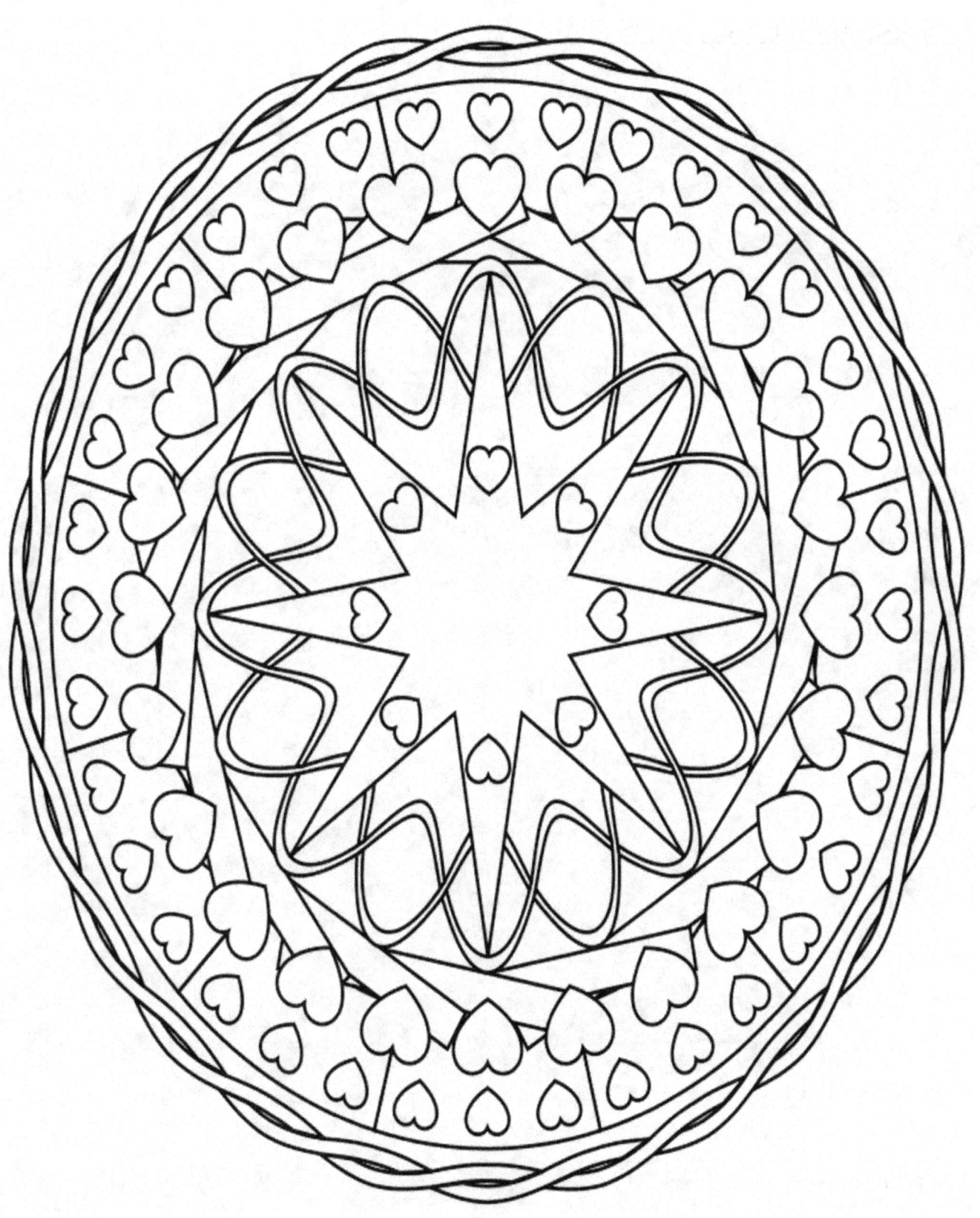

When strife fills the land?

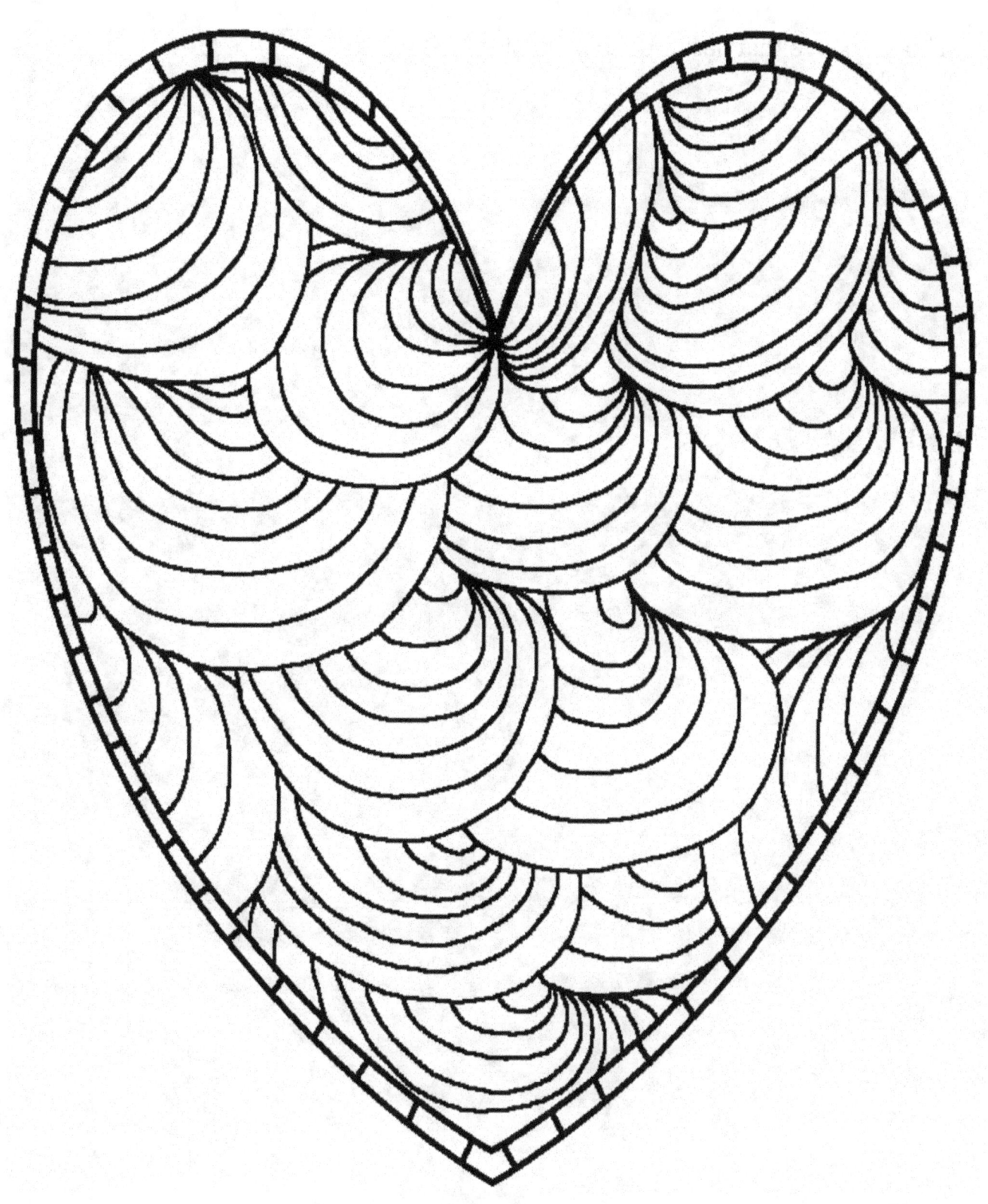

I choose a love that has hopeful beginnings,

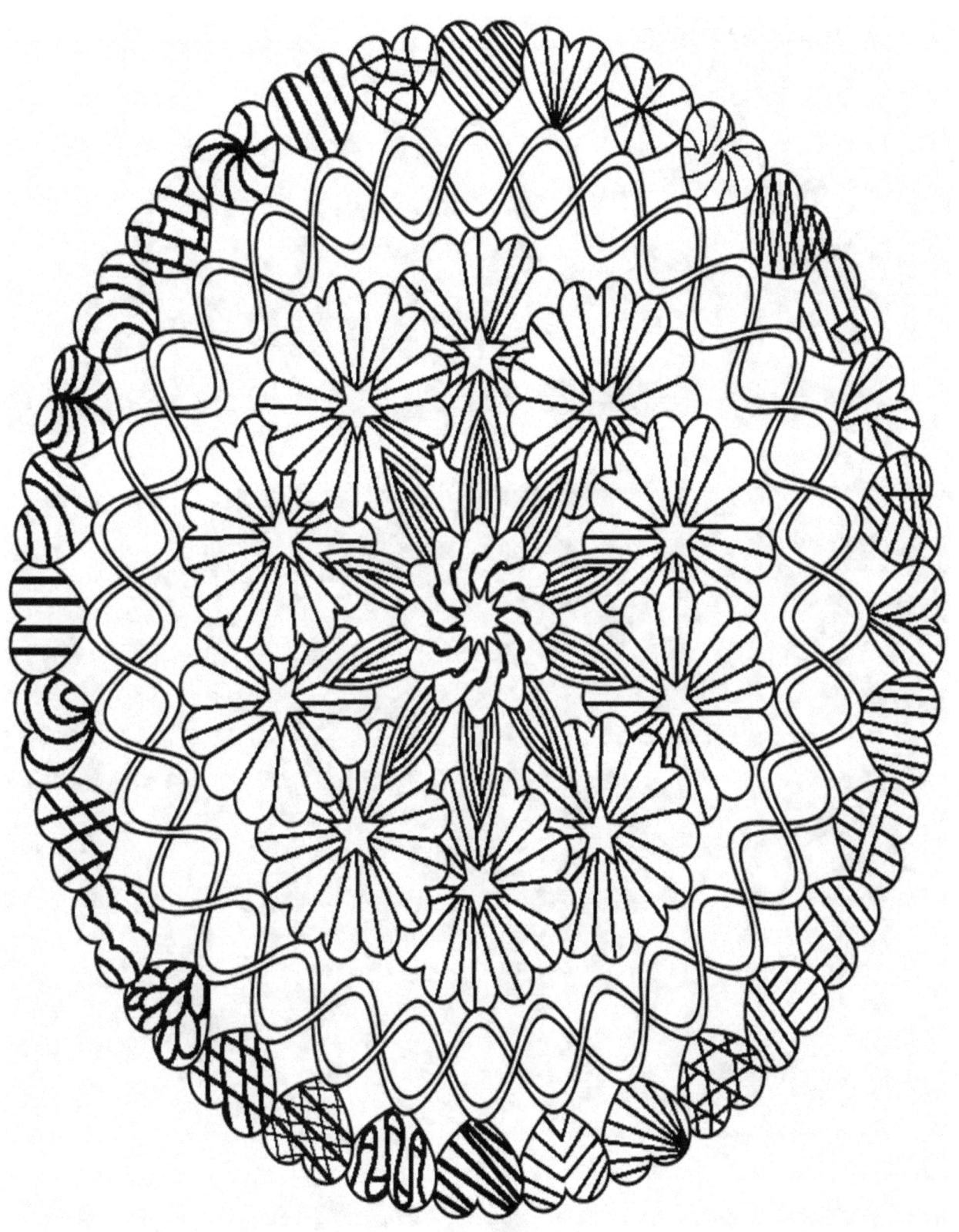

And a faith to see me through,

Old things are changed to new,

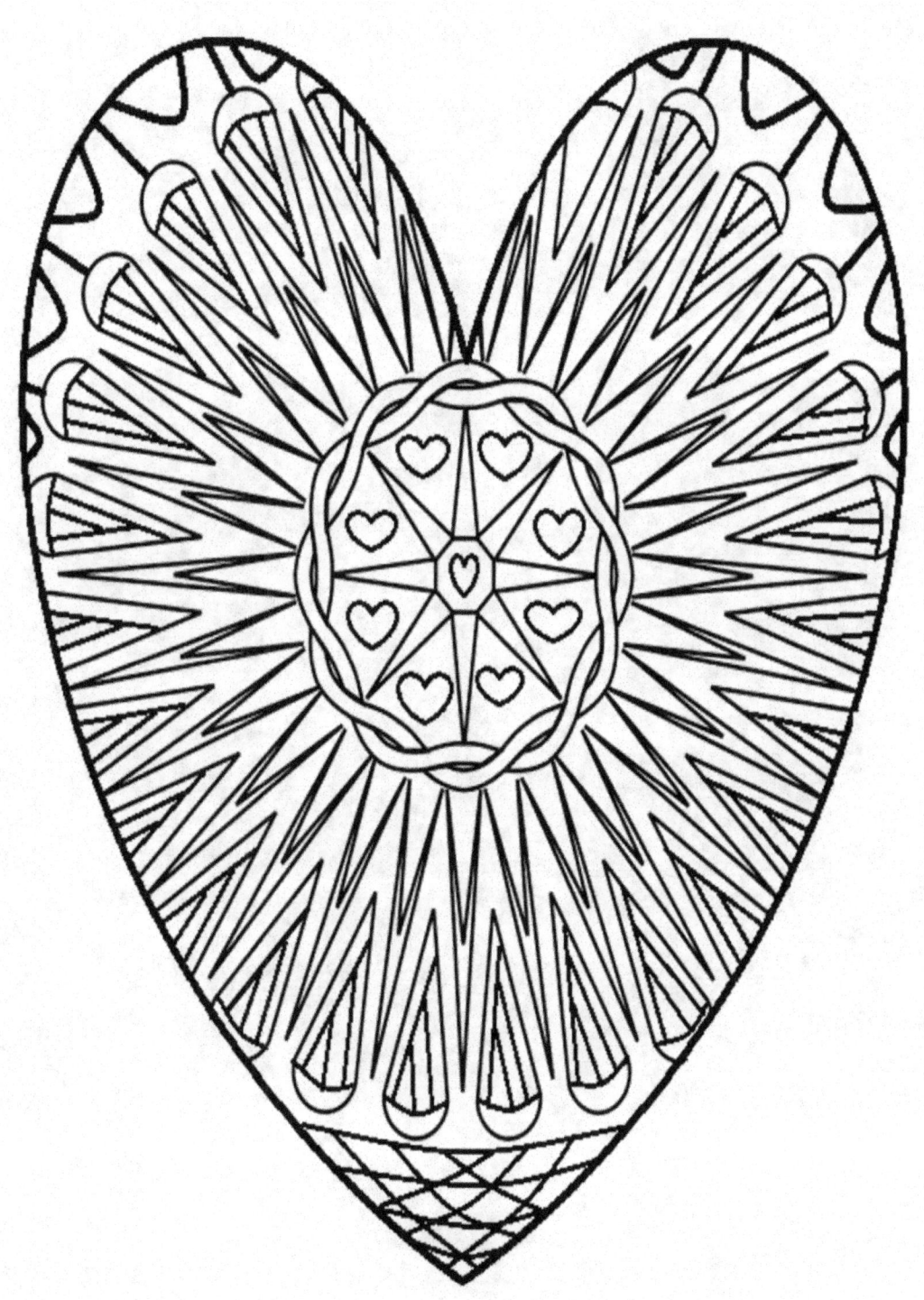

And even a child understands.

It's a powerful faith and hope and love.

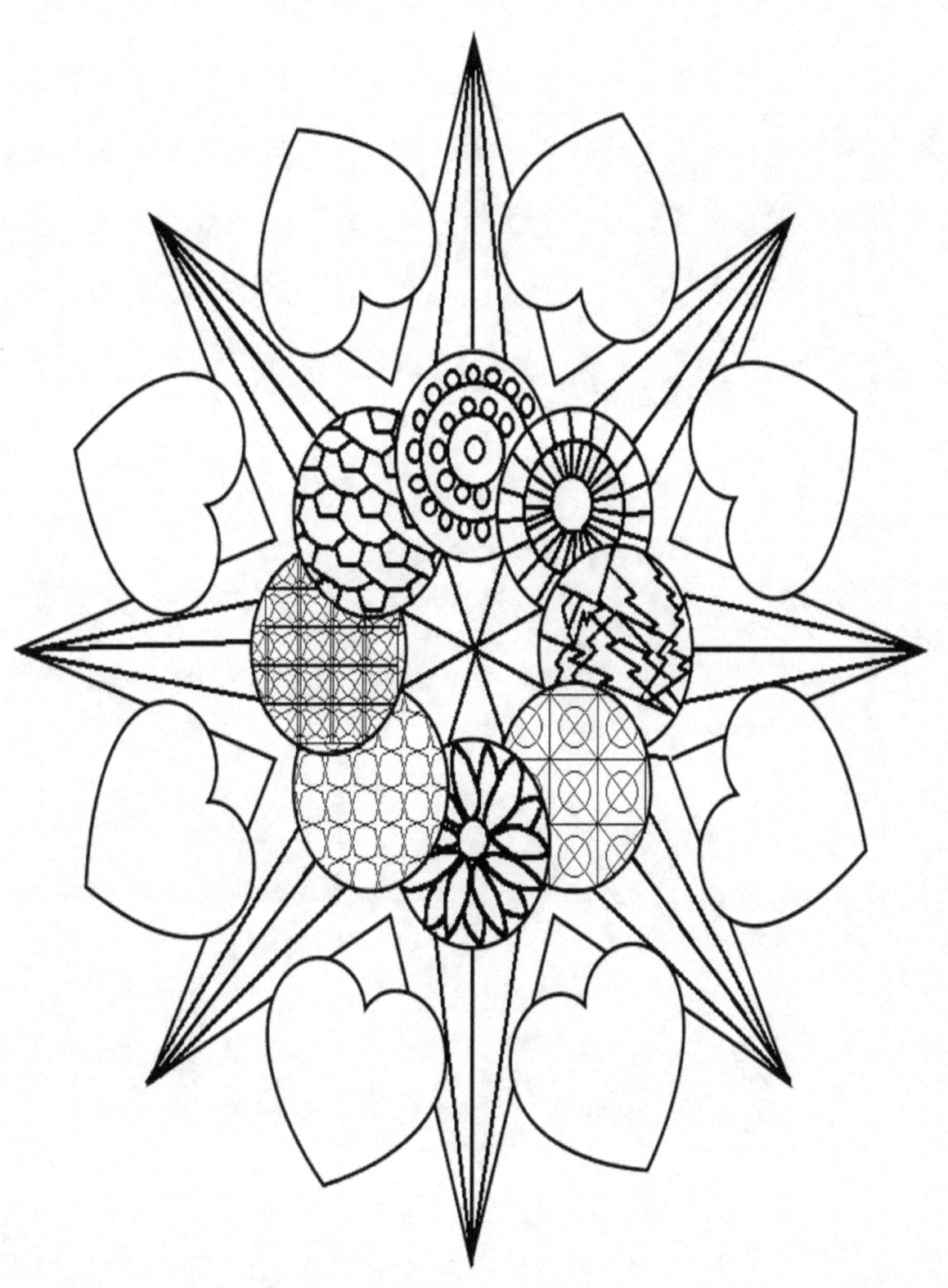

Got to understand that faith and hope and love.

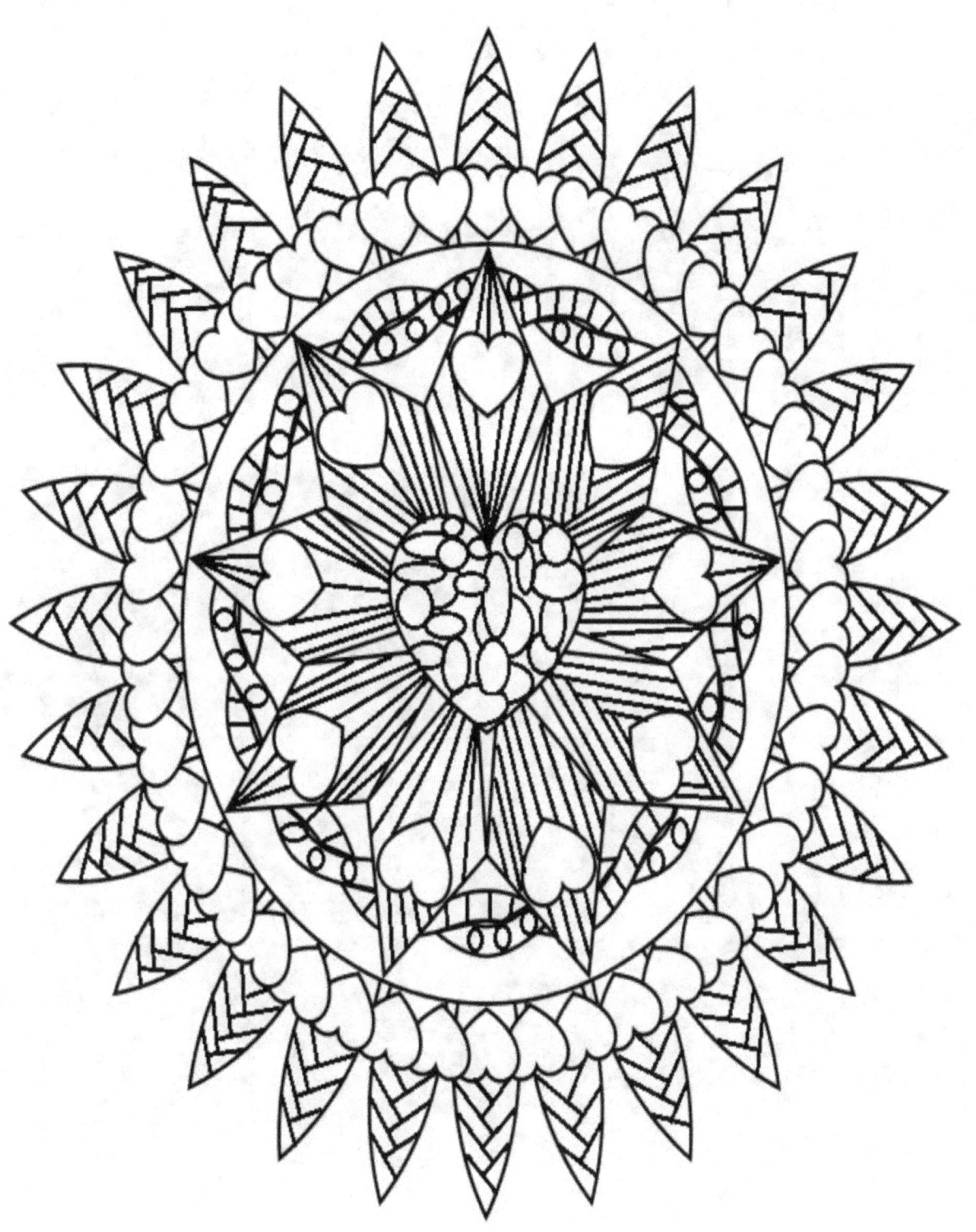

Got to focus on that faith and hope and love.

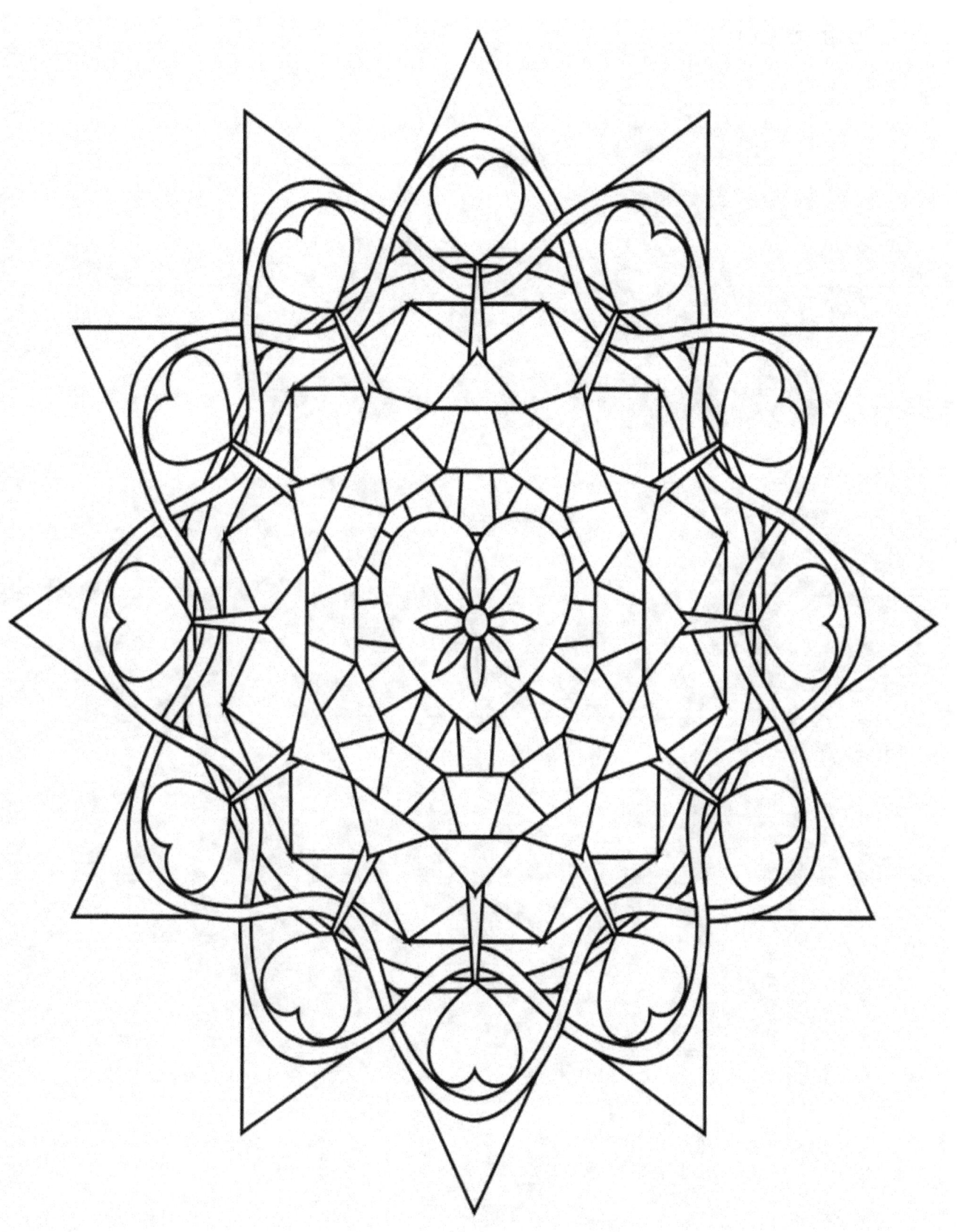

But the greatest is love,

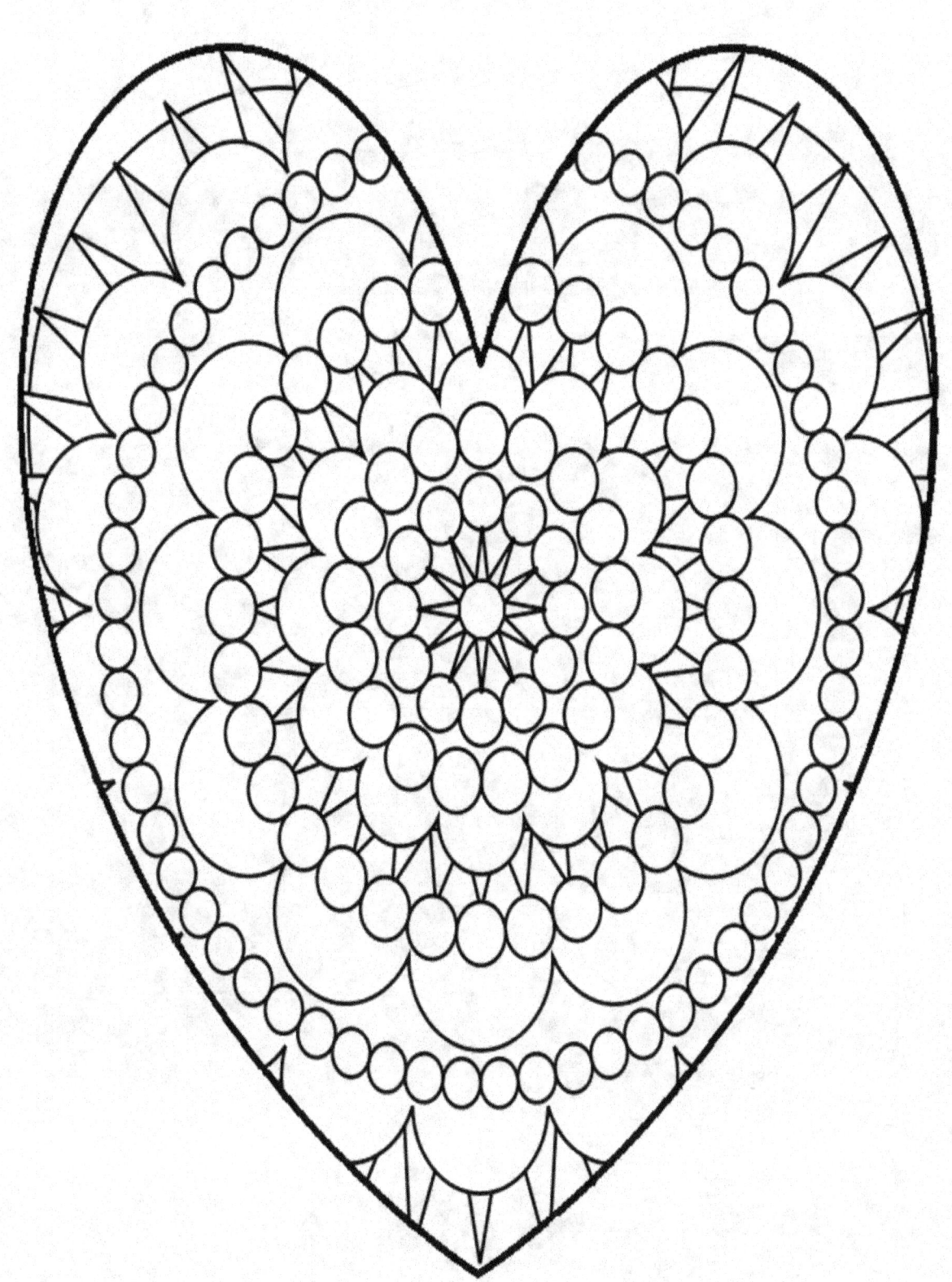

It's a wonderful love.

www.ingramcontent.com/pod-product-compliance
Lightning Source LLC
Chambersburg PA
CBHW081203180526
45170CB00006B/2193